# NEVER TRUST A LEADER WITHOUT A LIMP

## THE WIT AND WISDOM OF JOHN WIMBER FOUNDER OF THE **VINEYARD CHURCH MOVEMENT**

### GLENN SCHRODER

EMANATE
BOOKS

Published in Nashville, Tennessee, by Emanate Books, an imprint of Thomas Nelson. Emanate Books and Thomas Nelson are registered trademarks of HarperCollins Christian Publishing, Inc.

Thomas Nelson titles may be purchased in bulk for educational, business, fund-raising, or sales promotional use. For information, please e-mail SpecialMarkets@ThomasNelson.com.

Unless otherwise noted, Scripture quotations are taken from the Holy Bible, New International Version®, NIV®. Copyright © 1973, 1978, 1984, 2011 by Biblica, Inc.® Used by permission of Zondervan. All rights reserved worldwide. www.Zondervan.com. The "NIV" and "New International Version" are trademarks registered in the United States Patent and Trademark Office by Biblica, Inc.®

Scripture quotations marked NASB are from New American Standard Bible®. Copyright © 1960, 1962, 1963, 1968, 1971, 1972, 1973, 1975, 1977, 1995 by The Lockman Foundation. Used by permission. (www.Lockman.org)

Scripture quotations marked NLT are from the Holy Bible, New Living Translation. © 1996, 2004, 2007, 2013, 2015 by Tyndale House Foundation. Used by permission of Tyndale House Publishers, Inc., Carol Stream, Illinois 60188. All rights reserved.

Any Internet addresses, phone numbers, or company or product information printed in this book are offered as a resource and are not intended in any way to be or to imply an endorsement by Thomas Nelson, nor does Thomas Nelson vouch for the existence, content, or services of these sites, phone numbers, companies, or products beyond the life of this book.

ISBN 978-0-7852-3133-2 (eBook)
ISBN 978-0-7852-3131-8 (TP)

**Library of Congress Control Number: 2019952422**

*Printed in the United States of America*
20 21 22 23 24   LSC   10 9 8 7 6 5 4 3 2 1

# CONTENTS

# CONTENTS

O my people, listen to my instructions.
     Open your ears to what I am saying,
     for I will speak to you in a parable.
I will teach you hidden lessons from our past—
     stories we have heard and known,
     stories our ancestors handed down to us.
We will not hide these truths from our children;
     we will tell the next generation
about the glorious deeds of the Lord,
     about his power and his mighty wonders.
For he issued his laws to Jacob;
     he gave his instructions to Israel.
He commanded our ancestors
     to teach them to their children,
so the next generation might know them—
     even the children not yet born—
     and they in turn will teach their own children.
So each generation should set its hope anew on God,
     not forgetting his glorious miracles
     and obeying his commands.
             **—PSALM 78:1–7** NLT

*It is my honor to dedicate this book to the current generation of young leaders and pastors who are out there "doin' the stuff." And to the those who are not yet born. Be bold. Be brave. Be courageous. Be yourself. Take risks. Finish well.*

# FOREWORD

In my slightly aging eighty-and-a-half-year-old mind, there remains bright and clear the memory of a select and beloved group of mostly teenagers that I think of as First Team. I will always love these guys. Always! They are the ones who sacrificed everything to join us in our quest to discover what God would do if we let him, if we didn't shut him down, if we trusted him and obeyed him and got out of his way. Young and old, we were all taught by the Holy Spirit how to hear his voice, how to risk looking foolish, and how it is so important to obey in that moment of time when the Kingdom breaks through. Glenn Schroder and his wife, Donna, were with us from the very beginning. Glenn, like the rest of us on First Team, has seen and experienced more than he will ever be able to record in one book. But what he has recalled in these pages captures beautifully the essential truths and principles born out of the ministry of my late husband, John Wimber. I do so appreciate his taking the time and making the effort to write it down.

Thanks, Glenn!
Carol Wimber

# INTRODUCTION

John Richard Wimber was my pastor for twenty years and my boss for thirteen. Our relationship began in 1976 when I started attending a little home group in Yorba Linda, California, that eventually became the Anaheim Vineyard. I had the privilege of traveling with John on multiple occasions, as well as seeing him at home in a casual setting. He lived a unique life, had a unique calling, and was a unique leader. I loved him deeply and felt loved by him.

John, or JRW as those who knew him liked to refer to him, was born in the rural Midwest into a family of farmers but became an accomplished musician at a young age. Providentially, John's family relocated to California when he was twelve years old. Southern California proved to be more fertile soil for an aspiring musician than Missouri. He led his band at Anaheim High School in the Rose Parade and continued to develop his musical prowess, eventually connecting with a group called the Paramours that later became the Righteous Brothers. All was going well until he encountered a man named Gunner Payne.

Gunner was an oilfield worker and evangelist who had rough hands and a soft heart. Gunner's teenage daughter had been sexually assaulted and brutally murdered by a developmentally disabled itinerant farmhand.[1] Gunner turned the pain and tragedy of that event into a life of sharing Christ with others. He understood faith and forgiveness and passed those beliefs on to his disciples, including John Wimber. John was converted under Gunner's ministry in 1963 and left the music business, narrowly escaping going on tour with the Beatles. (The Righteous Brothers were selected by the Beatles to be their opening act on their first US tour in 1964.)

John began doing what he had been taught, sharing his faith. Over the next several years, he led hundreds of people to Christ and was leading multiple Bible studies, which opened the door to a position on staff at his church, Yorba Linda Friends. As an outcome of John's ministry, Yorba Linda became the fastest growing church in that denomination in the country. This turn led to John's being given a position as the director of the Department of Church Growth at Fuller Seminary.

His work at Fuller allowed John to travel the country and see both what was right and what was wrong with the church in America. He was often disillusioned by the focus on celebrity preachers and by big churches lacking depth, conviction, and commitment to care for the poor and needy in their communities. Meanwhile, John's wife, Carol; her sister, Penny Fulton; Penny's husband, Bob; Carl Tuttle; and a handful of others at the Friends Church were going through their own crisis of faith. They were self-proclaimed "burned-out Pharisees" and certain that there was more to following Jesus than what they were experiencing. They just didn't know what it was or quite how to find it. They began a little prayer and worship group on Sunday nights at Carl's sister's home across the street from the church and just began singing simple songs to Jesus and praying for more of his presence.

Before long the group grew, and ultimately the Lord led John home to pastor it.[2] A short time later the group officially became a church with John as the lead pastor and Bob Fulton and Carl Tuttle as associates. John would teach through the Gospels and the stories would come to life. He understood the power of story and was a master storyteller. He loved to make facial expressions and become animated as he talked about people disbelieving the things Jesus did or about the encounter with the Holy Spirit at Pentecost.

John took the work of George Eldon Ladd on the kingdom of God and communicated it so that it not only made sense to the whole congregation but had real-life and real-time application. Those of us present in the early days of the Vineyard began to believe that we could enter God's kingdom and participate in a meaningful way.

John's teaching became increasingly influential outside of the Vineyard movement as well. In the October 6, 2006, issue of *Christianity Today*, his book *Power Evangelism* was listed as the twelfth most influential book shaping evangelicalism in the twentieth century, saying, "These are books that have shaped evangelicalism as we see it today—not an evangelicalism we wish and hope for . . . books that over the last 50 years have altered the way American evangelicals pray, gather, talk, and reach out—not books that merely entertained."[3]

In addition to writing, John had another gift as well. He could share theological truth in pithy, memorable little sayings—Wimberisms. These were short statements of a truth or a life principle that were easy to remember and assimilate: "The meat's in the street," "The way in is the way on," and "Doin' the stuff." These little phrases are the essence of this book. Several years ago I began writing down as many Wimberisms as I could remember. I added a few things John had said to me personally, a bit about working with him, and some of John's teachings that seemed to best illustrate the truths behind his sayings.

The Vineyard movement is over forty years old now. Many of the original pastors are in the process of retiring or already have. Since I have opportunity to travel to Vineyard churches across the country as well as throughout Mexico and Central America, I interact more and more with people who never met John or heard him speak. Recently I had the chance to share at Project Timothy, a youth training program sponsored by the Vineyard Youth Task Force, and I discovered that I was the first person that any of the twenty-five young people in attendance had ever met who had met John personally.

It's been said, "If you forget your story, you lose your identity." So much of the story of the Vineyard movement comes from who John was and his convictions about how we are to live as followers of Christ. My prayer is that this collection of the "wit and wisdom" of John Wimber will both capture the essence of John's beliefs and teaching and help preserve the identity of the movement he started.

# FIRST IMPRESSIONS

I graduated from El Dorado High School in 1976. Throughout high school I had attended the youth group of a Presbyterian church in Placentia, California, where we lived. It was there that I received Christ and began my walk with the Lord. However, after graduation I found the transition into the adult congregation a bit rough. I was a true child of the seventies with long hair, a burly beard, and overalls. Shoes were optional.

The folks at Placentia Presbyterian were kind and loving people, but they also wore suits and ties to church. That, along with all the liturgical formalities—stand up, read this prayer, sit down, stand up, sing this song—made it difficult for me to fit in. I began to wander a bit until one evening later that summer.

My friend Mark Hill and his brother Keith had a pool table in their garage. It was our custom to open the door, shoot pool, and hang out. Anyone from school or other friends who drove by would see us out there, stop by, and join the party.

One night a friend of Keith's, Dan Roach, came by. We all had dirt bikes, and Keith and Dan often rode together. Dan attended Yorba Linda Friends Church and was part of an off-road riding club they had called Barney's Bikers—named after the pastor, Barney Schaeffer. John Wimber had been the associate pastor at the church for several years.

At that time I didn't know any of these people. Dan started to tell us about this little group that was meeting across the street from the church after the Sunday evening service. As he talked, this weird notion popped into my head: I should go to that group. I didn't know anyone there, except Dan, and he was just a friend of my friend's older brother. But all week the thought was pervasive: I really needed to go to that group! I realize now that thought was from the Holy Spirit, but at the time I had no grid for understanding that. As much as I had learned at the Presbyterian church, there was never any mention of the Holy Spirit, spiritual gifts, or anything of that nature. Other than the words to some of the hymns we sang, I would have thought they believed in the Holy Binity: Father and Son.

Sunday night arrived. I got in my car and drove to Yorba Linda. I knew where the church was, and as I pulled, up I thought, "There's a house across the street with a bunch of cars parked out front. This must be the place!" I walked in and was greeted warmly by several people. Right away I felt at home. Many of them were my age and dressed similarly to me.

After a few minutes a guy with long hair and a beard stepped into the room carrying a guitar in one hand and a wooden stool in the other. I learned later that his name was Carl Tuttle. *I've found my people*, I thought. I was used to the formality of the Presbyterian Church, and this was the polar opposite.

No one said anything—no opening prayer or "Take your seats." Carl just sat down and started strumming. That was the signal. Everyone gathered around. Some sat on couches, others on the floor. A few stood and started singing. I wasn't accustomed to one song going directly into the next, but that was the protocol here.

After about two or three songs, something strange happened to me. I began to cry. I didn't know why; I wasn't particularly sad or happy, but something emotional was happening deep inside me, and I couldn't stop crying. I was embarrassed and thought, *These people are going to think I'm nuts!* But as I glanced around through my tears, I realized no one was paying any attention to me. Most people had their eyes closed, and the rest seemed to be oblivious. Good.

After what seemed like hours (although I knew it wasn't), the singing stopped, and I was able to regain my composure. Then an older man who seemed very kind and pastoral (Bob Fulton) stood up and said, "Now we're going to break into groups and pray." That seemed easy enough, but there were no further instructions, and I wondered how the group system worked. Did I take a number? Should I go to a certain room? After a few seconds, I realized several people had gathered around me. I was in a group.

Someone asked, "Would you like us to pray for you?"

"Sure," I replied.

He said, "What would you like prayer for?" This second question was harder. I had no idea what I wanted prayer for. He smiled and said, "That's okay. We'll just pray."

I closed my eyes, and someone put their hand on my shoulder.

This seemed very natural, although in my experience you didn't touch people when praying for them. I don't recall anything that was prayed, but I do recall the most beautiful sense of peace and well-being coming over me. I believe it was John Wesley who described his initial experience with the Holy Spirit as warmth and liquid love. That's as good a description as I can think of. It was overwhelming and one of the most beautiful experiences I have ever had even to this day. As I drove home that night, I remember thinking, *I have no idea what just happened, but whatever it was, I have to have more of that.*

I attended the little—but rapidly growing—group every week after that. It became the highlight of my life. A few weeks later, during one of our meetings, there was a kind of murmuring in the group. I heard several people say, "John Wimber's here." Having never attended Yorba Linda Friends, I had no idea who John Wimber was, but many of them did. All I knew was that it must mean something important that he was there. I remember looking across the room and seeing this big, heavyset guy in a chair, with his arms crossed and a grumpy look on his face. My first impression was, *Who is John Wimber, and why is he so mad?* If you've heard John's testimony, this was the night his wife asked what he thought as they drove home, and John replied, "It's not going anywhere. There's no leader." Joke's on you, big guy.

Not long after that, Bob stood up one night and announced that through much prayer they had decided that the group was going to become a church. Everyone would need to decide if they wanted to stay at their current church or join this group. He also announced that he, John, and Carl would be the pastors.

It was a no-brainer for me. This was already my church. However, for many others this presented a challenging and potentially painful decision. Do you permanently leave the church in which you had been nurtured to join this little upstart group, or do you stay and let go of what you had been experiencing on Sunday nights with this new community of believers? At the time, as a nineteen-year-old who had recently encountered the Holy Spirit, this was exciting news. But now, in retrospect, I realize that this kind of decision is never easy. There is always a tearing and pain in following the Lord in a new direction. Though I wasn't directly involved, I know that Barney and the leaders of Yorba Linda Friends honored John and the new group and sent them off with a blessing. I believe this was not only the right thing to do but that God blessed them for it. That church has prospered ever since and is a thriving congregation of several thousand today.

As for the little upstart group, we had no place to meet and were scheduled to gather in the park on Mother's Day of 1977 for our first service. As it turned out, there was an unseasonal Southern California rainstorm that week. At the last minute it was announced that we would meet in the Masonic Lodge above the hardware store on Main Street in Yorba Linda. There were just over one hundred people that first Sunday.

After the service, I told John how glad I was to be part of what was happening and that if there was anything I could do to help, I would. Seven years later John hired me to be the youth pastor at Anaheim Vineyard and said, "On our first Sunday you told me that you'd do anything you could to help out, and you always have. Thanks for that." John valued loyalty and from time to time shared a "word in season" that meant a lot to us who served under him.

# CHAPTER 2

# THE MEAT IS IN THE STREET

*Now that you know these things, you will
be blessed if you do them.*
—JOHN 13:17

One of John's best-known phrases is "The meat is in the street."
One of my earliest memories after I began attending Vineyard
illustrates the meaning of that sentence. I was working as a gardener sometime around 1977 or 1978. My friend Chris and I
took a side job one Saturday trimming trees for a guy in Yorba
Linda. It proved to be a long day and hard work, but we made
good money and at the end of the day wanted to celebrate. The
nicest restaurant that was likely to welcome two gardeners still

in work clothes and dirty from head to toe was Sizzler. A steak sounded good, so off we went.

Not long after ordering, I heard a loud wheezing noise coming from the table next to us. I glanced over to notice three elderly people: two women and one man. The gentleman wheezed loudly again, causing several other patrons to also glance his way.

Chris and I had the same thought, at the same time, but neither of us wanted to say anything. We were tired, we were dirty, we looked like anything but ministers or faith healers or anyone remotely spiritual. After a few more wheezing episodes, Chris looked at me and said, "Do you think we should pray for him?"

We began to develop a strategy, but the approach was simple. We just needed to go over and ask if we could pray for the man. Finally we got up and approached the table. I said, "Excuse me, but we are Christians and believe God can heal people. We were wondering if possibly it would be okay to pray for you."

The gentleman looked a bit bewildered, but his wife immediately responded, "Oh yes, please do!" And so, in Sizzler with a number of customers looking on, two scraggly, dirty gardeners laid hands on an elderly man and began to ask the Lord to heal him. After a few minutes, during which the wheezing stopped, we concluded our prayer and thanked the group for letting us pray.

The other woman, who I learned was his wife's sister, tugged on my sleeve and said, "Pray for her too. She's got the arthritis real bad."

I looked directly at the woman. "Is that true?"

She sheepishly nodded and I said, "Okay, we're gonna pray for you too." She nodded again, and we began to pray. After a few minutes we concluded our impromptu prayer time, thanked these precious folks, and went back to our steak dinner.

I don't know what that man's condition was or if he was ultimately completely healed. I never saw him after that night. What I do know is that for the remainder of our time in the restaurant the wheezing had stopped. I also know that those people felt loved and encouraged and that Chris and I experienced the joy of the Lord that comes from being obedient and allowing him to use us for his kingdom purposes.

The phrase "the meat is in the street" originated after a worship service at the Anaheim Vineyard when a woman approached John and asked, "When are we going to get into the meat?"

He politely replied, "Excuse me?"

"You know," she continued. "The meat of the Word. When are we going to get into the meat?"

John replied, "The meat is in the street!"

While it is a catchy little phrase, "the meat is in the street" also summarizes what John considered the Bible's greatest value for daily living. He believed that we were to read the Word, study the Word, meditate on the Word, memorize the Word, *and* put it into practice!

The Vineyard began during a time when the evangelical church in America placed considerable emphasis on knowing the Word of God. Spirituality was often measured by how many Bible studies a week a person went to. Knowing the Word was the goal and an end in itself. John's position was that knowing the Word wasn't enough, that the Scripture meant something only when a person put it into practice. Hence, *the meat is in the street*.

This is referring, of course, to the passage in 1 Corinthians 3, in which Paul told the church that they were mere infants in the Spirit, not yet ready for solid food, so he gave them milk. Paul was referring to their behavior, their actions. They weren't living out the things they had learned. The same is true of the corollary passage in Hebrews 5. The Hebrew church hadn't learned to distinguish good from evil. Apparently Paul and the writer of Hebrews agreed with John. The meat, the depth of the Word, is in the application to our lives. God's desire for his people is that they, the body of Christ, would be the continuation of Jesus and his ministry in the world. He never intended for us to simply know the Word. He intends for us to live the Word. Our very purpose is to carry out the words and works of Jesus where we live.

It doesn't have the same ring to it, but it's worth mentioning that the phrase isn't "The meat is in the church." It's in the street. If our entire Christian experience consists of going to worship, attending Bible study, and fellowshipping with our brethren, we will also miss out on the meat—the solid food of the Word. Jesus instructed his followers to make disciples of all nations (Matt. 28). In Acts 1 his instructions are to be witnesses in Jerusalem, where they were currently, then to go to Judea, Samaria, and ultimately to the ends of the earth. Just as the Word isn't intended to be only learned and studied, the outworking isn't intended only for the confines of the Christian community.

One of the things I've always appreciated about the Vineyard is that from the onset the focus has always been on getting out of the building and taking the aroma of Christ to the world around us. In 1982 my wife and I were part of a team sent out by the Anaheim Vineyard to Johannesburg, South Africa, to plant the first Vineyard church in South Africa (actually anywhere on the continent of Africa). We ultimately spent almost two months there, but for the first several weeks our job was to meet people. To meet people, make friends, and talk to them about Jesus.

This was (and I don't say this often) a life-changing experience. We learned to get out and intentionally share our faith. To take what we believed and live it out in real-life situations. My wife, Donna, met a woman named Lea, who had suffered from anorexia nervosa throughout much of her young life. As we got to know Lea and her friends, opportunities presented themselves to minister to her—to share the love of Christ and pray for her.

After a few weeks of simply living the meat in the street, we were joined by John, Lonnie Frisbee, Blaine Cook, and a team of pastors. We held several meetings, to which we invited the people we'd been meeting. After a time of worship, John would teach on the kingdom and then we'd have a ministry time and pray for healing.

During one of these meetings, John had a word of knowledge that God wanted to fill teeth. Before the meeting, our team had met with John and he shared that he believed God would do miracles that night. Donna walked away praying, "Lord, I want to see a miracle!"

There were many lower-income people in attendance who couldn't afford regular dental care, and there was a huge response to the word. One gentleman, who appeared well off, came forward. He was an Afrikaans man, wearing slacks and a sport coat. My nineteen-year-old bride and I asked to pray with him, and he explained that he had no teeth in the back of his mouth and believed that God would give him new teeth.

My first reaction was, *That wasn't the word*. The word was for *fillings* not *new teeth*. My second reaction was, *This is way above my pay grade*. However, my lovely faith-filled wife immediately responded that she would pray for him. I'm not sure who suggested it, but the idea was floated that she should put her fingers in his mouth, "lay hands" on his gums, and pray. She stands all of five foot, one inch and had to literally get on her tiptoes. This was now not only above my pay grade but way out of my comfort zone.

After praying for just a minute or two, Donna and the man screamed simultaneously. I thought, *My God, he bit her!* But what happened was that they both felt popping in his mouth as new teeth formed. Minutes later she ran over to tell Carol what had happened. Carol's response was like that of a mother looking at her toddler: "Well, what do you know? The Vineyard's first tooth!"

Over the years the Enemy has a way of creeping in and sowing doubt: Did that really happen? We were in several Vineyard meetings and conferences over the years when someone (usually John) shared that story. Donna would always say, "Oh, no, not the tooth story." We both wondered what had really happened. It seemed so long ago, so distant, so unreal.

In 1997 we attended the twentieth anniversary celebration of the Anaheim Vineyard. Our old friend Costa Mitchell, the pastor of the Johannesburg Vineyard, was one of those asked to speak. Costa began to talk about how his church started, back in 1982, when a group of young Californians came and shared their faith in the streets of Johannesburg. Then he said that not long ago a man came up to him and asked, "You're Costa Mitchell, pastor of the Vineyard?"

"Yes, I am," he replied.

The man said, "I've been looking for you for a long time. In 1982 I was at a meeting of your church, and a little American girl put her fingers in my mouth and prayed that God would give me new teeth, and he did. I've been wanting to tell you thank you. My life hasn't been the same since."

Another of John's sayings was "Believe your beliefs and doubt your doubts." We'll look at that a little more later, but for now just remember that when the Enemy comes in and sows doubt, it's a lie. What's true is Jesus, his Word, and the reality that the meat really is in the street.

# CHAPTER 3

# EVERYBODY GETS TO PLAY

*You also, like living stones, are being*
*built into a spiritual house to be a holy*
*priesthood, offering spiritual sacrifices*
*acceptable to God through Jesus Christ.*
—1 PETER 2:5

In 1991 I received a phone call. The youth pastor of a church in Modesto, California, asked if I would be willing to speak at a citywide youth conference he was holding. During our conversation, I asked if they had a worship leader and team lined up. He replied that they hoped to but were in the early stages of planning. I told him I would be happy to come and speak but would prefer to bring a worship team and ministry team with me, to which he replied, "That would be great!" So it was set. Neither of us realized that five-minute conversation would significantly disrupt the flow of things in his church.

During the conference a few of the young adults from our team gave words of knowledge, prayed for people, and engaged in ministry. The attendees were from several area churches, and while it was a little unusual for them to hear young lay people giving words of knowledge, overall the young adults didn't present too big of a disparity. However, the Sunday morning service proved to be a different story.

The conference went well, so the pastor invited our team to stay and lead their Sunday service. Everything was fine until the end of the message. I entered a ministry time and invited people to come forward for prayer. Instead of just coming forward, they formed a single-file line, waiting for me to pray for them.

This was how ministry was done in their tradition. The pastor did the ministry; he prayed for each person. Unfortunately, our team consisted of young people who had never seen this done before. Their only frame of reference was that the entire ministry team, composed of anyone with training, could and did pray. Consequently, they began engaging people who were waiting, asking what they could pray for. A few young people were politely told no, but others were welcomed to pray.

While we had already inadvertently breached protocol, things got worse when Mike, a young musician on our team, prayed for an older man in line who almost immediately fell over in the Spirit. The senior pastor, whom I had not yet met, and the youth pastor both looked at me with a bit of concern. Our young people had been taught that "everybody gets to play." They had never known anything else. At this point there was nothing I could do to retrieve our team and restore order. While I was reluctant to show any disrespect to the church's practice, I had not been told of the protocol beforehand, and the Holy Spirit was honoring our team's prayers and ministry. I began to pray for people in line but didn't discourage others from praying.

Afterward we went to lunch with the youth pastor, who had several questions about what he'd seen. I was explaining our ministry philosophy when he asked, "So, other people actually give words of knowledge and prophecies?"

"Of course," I replied.

With a look of fear, he asked, "Are they ever wrong?"

Laughing out loud, I said, "Ah, yeah, sometimes they're wrong."

"What do you do then?"

"Well, we simply evaluate, learn, and move on. Maybe they missed it. Maybe the person the word was for didn't acknowledge it or wasn't aware themselves. But it isn't a failure, just a learning experience."

I was never invited back. However, my conviction, instilled in me from many years of John's teaching and practice, plus my personal experience, was that ministry is not only for professionals, the spiritually elite, or the wise and learned. It is truly for everyone.

John is remembered by many people for his healing ministry. I believe that his greatest contribution to the church, however, was putting ministry back into the hands of the people. During the latter portion of the twentieth century, the model for ministry in many Pentecostal or Charismatic churches was that the professionals did the ministry. They laid on hands, prayed for healing, cast out demons, and performed other "priestly" functions.

From the time I was eighteen and began attending the little group that eventually became the Anaheim Vineyard, I had been taught something very different. The approach modeled for me showed that no one was too young or too old, or too young in the Lord, to begin learning how to minister to others. Every person has a valuable and vital contribution to make. While some are more comfortable in a spectator's role, most people want to contribute. They want to make a difference. John led the way in teaching us that we could.

To have purpose is a longing in every heart. To have kingdom purpose is a longing in every kingdom heart. When we say "everybody gets to play," we are saying that you, too, have a purpose. What you bring to the table is a unique contribution that no one else can make. Each of us is uniquely created by God with our own personality and blend of perspectives and gifts.

John put it this way:

From the onset we operated with the supposition that what we were doing was for everybody. We believed Ephesians 4:11–12. God has given to the church: apostles, prophets, evangelists, pastors, and teachers "for the equipping of the saints for the work of service" (NASB). Either by teaching Bible studies, running home groups, doing pastoral counseling, or doing evangelistic work, everyone is supposed to learn to do ministry. I learned through experience that the kingdom premise, "You get to keep only that which you give away," is true. I already knew that through evangelism you gave away your faith, and your faith was sharpened in the process. I knew that by teaching you gave away the things that had nurtured you, and in the process you were replenished. I found out the same thing was true in the leadership dimension: I had to give my leadership away to see it multiplied and spread.[1]

I often say to people in our congregation who have missed a Sunday or two, "It isn't the same here without you." They smile and think I'm just being nice, but I truly mean it. It isn't the same. No one else is you. No one else can give what you give. At this point I would say that not only does everybody get to play but that everybody is needed. The body of Christ is incomplete without the contribution that each person was created and designed to bring.

In the early days of the Vineyard (then called Calvary Chapel), when Donna was only fifteen years old, she was a part of the ministry team. One Sunday night a woman came forward for prayer. Donna and her sister Cheryl approached her and asked what they could pray for. She responded, "Oh, that's okay, nothing right now." The woman then approached Bob Fulton, our associate pastor, and reported that she had come for prayer, was approached by two young girls, and wondered if there was someone more experienced she could pray with.

Bob's response was, "Those two are some of the best prayer people we have. If they can't pray for you, there really isn't anyone else here who can." With humility, she came back to the girls and said, "I've just gone through a divorce and thought it might be better to pray with someone who could understand."

Donna's reply to her was, "I've been through a divorce too. My parents recently divorced. I think I understand." They shared a beautiful prayer time and wept together, after which she mentioned she couldn't fully straighten out her arm. The girls prayed again, and she was healed instantly.

Everybody gets to play.

# CHAPTER 4

---

# DOIN' THE STUFF

*Jesus told him, "Go and do likewise."*
—LUKE 10:37

The phrase "Doin' the stuff" comes from a conversation John had with a pastor shortly after his conversion. John naively asked, "When do we get to do the stuff?"

"What stuff?" came the response.

"You know, the stuff in the book: healing people and casting out demons. That stuff!"

"Oh, we don't do it. We just talk about it."[1]

John's pursuit of "the stuff," combined with his conviction that the Holy Spirit is active in our lives today and that the kingdom will come to earth as it is in heaven if we ask, led to thousands upon thousands of people being trained and engaged in kingdom ministry.

Shortly after Anaheim Vineyard began, Blaine Cook asked if I would like to join him in teaching a class on healing at another church. It was a four-week class during their adult Sunday school hour. "Sure, why not?" I said. So I joined Blaine, sitting in the front row, listening and watching as he led the class. One morning he was talking about spiritual gifts and specifically about the word of knowledge and how the Holy Spirit would speak to us and give us direction for ministry if we asked. Then, in classic Wimber "clinic time" style, he said, "Now, I'm going to pray that the Holy Spirit will speak to some of you and give you a word of knowledge for someone else in the room." Blaine prayed and we all waited quietly, listening intently as he had taught.

Almost immediately the thought popped into my head: *Someone here has a hormone imbalance.* It was a strange thought, and I surmised it must just be me. The thought persisted. The harder I tried not to think about a hormone imbalance, the more I thought about it. I tried my best to convince myself that it was just me making this up. It couldn't be a real word of knowledge. After several minutes of mental gyrations, I had the thought, *How often have you ever thought about a hormone imbalance?* Never. The answer was never. I could not remember a single occasion when I had ever thought about a hormone imbalance. So I raised my hand and told Blaine and the class that I felt someone might have a hormone imbalance. Immediately a woman in the back of the room waved her hand and shouted, "That's me, that's me!" She reported that she had been experiencing fatigue and a variety of other symptoms for weeks, she had finally gone to see her doctor, and he had diagnosed her with a hormone imbalance.

In that simple show-and-tell, "watch me and then do what I do" way, we all learned to do the stuff in the Book. In those early years I observed John, Carol, Blaine, and Becky and others pray for scores of people and cast out demons as well as receive and give multitudes of words of knowledge that led to others praying and engaging.

One of the responsibilities each of the pastoral staff at Anaheim had to take on was POC, or pastor on call. On our day, we handled any phone calls, people who walked in, or hospital visits. Early in my tenure I was POC, and we received a call to go to a local hospital and pray for an infant who had been born prematurely and was in the NICU. I showed up a short time later, and the family was happy and hopeful to see me. Little Christopher had been born several weeks early, weighing only a little over three pounds. His grandmother greeted me in the waiting room, gave me a little history, and then called the nurse, who opened the NICU door to let me in.

First, I had to scrub up and put on a surgical mask. This was a bit unnerving for me, as I've never liked hospitals, blood, needles—any of it. I followed the nurse into the area where the baby was being cared for. His mother was waiting. She, too, wore a surgical mask. I wasn't prepared for what I saw next. This tiny little body had so many needles, tubes, monitors, and other medical apparatus attached that there was almost no area of skin not connected to something.

I greeted his mother, and together we began to pray. After only a couple of minutes of prayer, I began to feel woozy and thought I was going to pass out. I excused myself and went back into the waiting area. I sat down for a minute to regain my composure, then found the grandmother and said goodbye. I drove home totally defeated and questioning whether I had made a mistake going into ministry at all. This wasn't fun.

Later that night Donna asked how my day was, and I told her about the experience. I broke down crying and said, "That baby is going to die." Over the next few days I recovered somewhat. I relied on John's teaching about healing—that it was our job to be obedient and pray and God's job to heal. I entrusted tiny little Christopher to the Lord and continued to pray for him.

Several weeks later I was walking down the hallway after a Sunday evening service. I was on my way to our daughter's classroom to pick her up and head home when a young woman ran up to me, grabbed me by the shirt, and said in a fairly loud voice, "I've been looking everywhere for you!"

I didn't recognize her and wasn't sure what I had done to garner this response. "Christopher is doing good. He's all right; he's coming home. God healed him!" I then realized this was the young mother from the NICU whom I had only seen wearing a surgical mask. Despite my own doubt and disappointment, God had indeed healed the little guy. I learned that prayer isn't contingent on our emotions or any physical sign or feeling. It really is in God's hands. He can and does heal even when we feel nothing. Maybe this wasn't such a bad gig after all.

There is one particular incident that I will always remember for another reason. John's life, teaching, and ministry continue to impact not only me but those I love and minister to. In September 2015 my twin grandchildren, birthed by a surrogate mother, were born at 23.6 weeks gestation, weighing one pound, one ounce and one pound, six ounces respectively. A team of neonatologists strongly suggested to my daughter and our family that we choose palliative care, meaning essentially to prepare to say goodbye. The chances of survival were very, very slim. We were also told that any birth occurring before twenty-four weeks was considered a fetus, not yet a baby. The terms used again and again were "morbid" and "extremely unlikely." We were also told that if the babies survived, they would have severe neurological defects.

When Jourdan (our daughter) came into the waiting room to tell us that the infants might not live through the night, I prayed, "Not today, Lord. Not today." That became my daily prayer over the ensuing three months that the twins—Jaxon Brave and Cadence Grace—were in the NICU. Each morning as I woke up, I'd say again, "Not today, Lord. Not today."

Until the twins' births, little Christopher had been the smallest baby I'd ever seen. These two were a third of his weight—so small they could fit in the palm of my hand. Yet despite any lack of feeling or faith on my part, Christopher was healed. Let me be clear. I am incredibly grateful to the medical community. As a Spirit-filled pastor who believes in divine healing, I am aware that God works in many ways, and that he has gifted men and women to bring healing through science and technology as well. I have friends and family members who are doctors, nurses, and other medical professionals. I am grateful and indebted to them for their service. We all believe that a combination of God's divine providence along with medical care brought healing and life to Jax and Cadence.

On New Year's Eve 2015, after ninety-eight days in the NICU, the twins came home. There were some difficulties, but they were both miraculously thriving. Today as I write, they are thirty months old and weigh twenty-seven pounds each. They crawl, stand, climb, jabber, and do most everything other toddlers their age do. Every so often when Cadence wakes up from her afternoon nap, she will tell her mom to "call Papa." I answer the FaceTime call, and there is my curly-haired granddaughter saying, "Hi, Papa!" and blowing me kisses. Thanks be to God! Thanks be to the amazing teams that took care of the twins and continue to, and thanks be to the hundreds—and thousands—of people who so diligently prayed for them.

Once a year Hollie, Jourdan's surrogate, joins Jourdan and Matt at the NICU reunion where all the previous NICU children from past years are invited back to see the doctors and nurses. Hollie asked our primary neonatologist if she had ever discharged another twenty-three-weeker before. She responded, "I don't think so—certainly never twins—and certainly no twenty-three-weekers doing so well. They are miracles."

# CHAPTER 5

# DON'T GO INTO MINISTRY
# UNLESS YOU CAN'T
# DO ANYTHING ELSE

*Besides everything else, I face daily the*
*pressure of my concern for all the churches.*
—2 CORINTHIANS 11:28

Pastoral ministry isn't easy. I cannot count the number of times I've said to myself over the years, "There must be a better way to make a living." Anyone who has been in ministry for any length of time and is honest will tell you the same thing. In a real way, being in pastoral ministry can be a spiritual liability. You set yourself up for disappointment, disillusionment, and criticism. In those difficult times it's imperative to remember why you got into this in the first place.

It's at those times that I am also grateful to John for telling me not to go into ministry unless I couldn't do anything else. As a zealous, passionate young Christian, I would think my pastor would do all he could to encourage me toward ministry. And John did. However, he never painted an unrealistic or overly rosy picture of what ministry would be like. Conversely, he was blunt and honest about it, telling eager young leaders like me, "Don't go into ministry unless you can't do anything else." What he meant was that if we had a clear sense of calling and conviction from the Lord and couldn't possibly envision our lives going any other direction, then, and only then, should we pursue ministry. John understood the practical realities of ministry—not only the disappointments but the time and energy commitment required.

I remember whining to John about how hectic my life was. Shortly after our first daughter was born, I was involved in a pastoral training program called Vineyard Institute for Ministry (VI today). We had classes two nights a week. I was working full time, my wife and I were leading a home group, and my responsibilities with the youth group were also growing. I told John that I was just too busy and that I couldn't possibly keep up with all of this. He looked at me, smiled, then said, "Welcome to the ministry."

I gave him that glazed-over, deer-in-the-headlights look, and he said, "This is what the rest of your life will be like if you choose to go into ministry: you will always be busy, most likely always be tired, and quite often be a little overwhelmed." He was right. I've been in pastoral ministry for thirty-four years and found that regardless of what season of life or stage of ministry we're in, it's always busy. Even a master delegator will find he or she has lots to do. Ministry seems to have a way of multiplying itself. In truth, it's just a busy lifestyle. If you're good at it, you'll be available to people, especially those in crisis. You work nights and weekends by default and probably wear multiple hats in the context of your local church. I like to tell young people who ask about what being in ministry is like, "This job is a lot of things, but it's not boring."

Donna and I have learned a lot in thirty-four years. We review our calendar monthly, plan ahead for family time, date nights, and vacations. We set boundaries and develop rhythms of life and ministry. But we've also let go of the myth that "once we get past this next season, things will slow down." We realize that our lives are busy. We've accepted and embraced that. Honestly, it's a joy to look back on the lives we've been able to impact, the opportunities we've had to experience God and to help others experience him as well. We wouldn't have it any other way. I don't want to look back on my life and think, "I wish I'd . . ."

Ministry isn't for everyone. An assurance of a genuine call is essential. If you're married, commitment from both spouses is absolutely essential. A willingness to live sacrificially is part of the deal.

But, if you can't do anything else, it's a pretty good use of your life.

# CHAPTER 6

# PUT YOUR SHOES AND SOCKS ON AND GO TO WORK

*Whatever you do, work at it with all your heart, as working for the Lord, not for human masters.*
—COLOSSIANS 3:23

John once said something to me that had a huge impact on my life as well as on the lives of others whom I've had the opportunity to share it with. In the early years of the church, before joining the staff, I was self-employed as a gardener. John was one of my long-standing clients. Every Friday I would pull up to his house in my old truck and take care of the lawn and landscaping.

Because of his travel and meeting schedule, I rarely saw John on these days.

However, one Friday I was struggling spiritually and emotionally. As I pulled in to the driveway and turned off the truck, out the front door walked John. He sauntered over, leaned on the truck door with his arms resting on the window ledge, and asked, "How's it going?"

I quickly launched into a lengthy discourse about all my woes and everything that was wrong. John listened patiently and then replied, "Well, you're doing the right thing."

"I am?" I queried.

"Yeah, you are. When you're having one of those days, what you feel like doing is staying in bed, pulling the covers over your head, and sucking your thumb. But what you need to do is get up, put your shoes and socks on, and go to work. Work and do what you need to do. Don't let it get the best of you. Then the Enemy wins. Go to work and pray in tongues, pray till it lifts. It might take a few minutes, or it might take all day, but it'll lift." Then he slapped me on the back, said "Have a good day," and walked back into the house.

Who was that masked man? John's words were not only a simple and straightforward answer to the dilemma I was in but also some of the best advice I've ever received. It was practical and spiritual all at the same time. Being naturally supernatural didn't just apply to giving words of knowledge or praying for the sick. It was a lifestyle.

John believed, and taught, that we walk in the Spirit and by the Spirit all the time. We follow the Spirit's leading while we are at work and school and home, not just in church. He was fiercely practical and understood the value of pressing in, not just to the Spirit but to the abundant life that Jesus has provided for us. That includes, of course, going to work. Carrying out our daily responsibilities and not hiding from or shirking them in the interest of self-absorption.

John didn't separate the sacred from the secular. In his mind, going to work was a spiritual discipline and just as much a weapon of spiritual warfare as praying in tongues. He understood that, in the process of combining the spiritual and the sacred, we would regain perspective and overcome any lie the Enemy might try to use to infiltrate our hearts and distract us from God's ultimate purpose in our lives.

He was right. I unloaded my lawn mower and began mowing and praying. I prayed in the spirit as I worked, and it wasn't long until the fog began to lift. While my circumstances hadn't changed, I managed to rise above them and find peace in the presence of God. I believe it was the combination of prayer and work that lifted my spirit that day. There is an inherent value in work. Since creation it has been evident that God's design is for man to work.

To work is a blessing and a privilege. It will bear fruit in our lives in personal self-worth and accomplishment. It will bear fruit in the lives of others in the resources that we can contribute. We should not look at the forty or more hours a week that we work as unredeemed time. Conversely, those hours are a gift from God and a part of his will being worked out in us.

Over the years I've had the opportunity to share this story with others. It has often had the same effect on them as it originally did on me. John's advice brings a new perspective on life and what we can do when life presents circumstances that challenge us.

So the next time the Enemy begins to get the best of you, don't pull the covers over your head and stay in bed all day. Get up, put your shoes and socks on, and go to work. And pray. Pray in tongues. It may take a few minutes, or it may take all day, but your spirit will lift.

# CHAPTER 7

# MINISTRY IS MORE CAUGHT THAN TAUGHT

*Follow my example, as I follow the example
of Christ.*
—1 CORINTHIANS 11:1

John often took a veritable gang of "sneaker-wearing, gum-chewing young Americans" as his ministry team on early trips to England and South Africa. He firmly maintained what he referred to as a "rabbinic model of discipleship." I called it show-and-tell. John knew that the practices of the kingdom would best be transferred not in a classroom setting but as people were encouraged to engage in the process. He also knew that there was no going back after someone tasted and experienced the presence of God working through them and learned that they could be genuine agents of healing, deliverance, and redemption.

That rang true for me. After high school I enrolled in the local community college (then called junior college) with the idea that I would do my time there, transfer to a university, get my degree and then my teaching credentials, and settle into a high school classroom somewhere. It seemed like a perfectly acceptable plan. Until one evening when my phone rang. It was Bob Fulton.

John was taking a team to England and wanted me to go. Bob explained the details and asked what I thought.

I told him it sounded great, but I had to work. I was gardening at the time, and although it was summer and classes were out, I needed to work as much as possible to save up extra cash for the school year. Bob tried to talk me into going and encouraged me to "really pray about it!"

A couple of days later I was working at the Wagner House (our church office building) when Penny Fulton came out to talk to me. "You need to go on this trip," she said. "It's a great opportunity, and God is going to do really good things." They were bringing out the big guns now. Penny twisted my arm for another twenty minutes or so, but again I said I had no one to cover the route for me and really needed to work. I just wouldn't be able to go.

Sunday mornings I was part of a crew that showed up at the high school early to roll out carpet, set up chairs, and get the gymnasium ready for worship. It was about 7:30 a.m., and we were already setting up when John walked in. He came directly over to me and said, "Hey, I hear you're going to England with us. That's great!"

"Well actually, John, I'm not gonna be able to go."

"That's funny," he replied. "I just saw your name on the list this morning, and it said 'confirmed.'" Then, in typical Wimber fashion, he smiled and walked away. So I was going to England. And though I didn't know it yet, that was the beginning of the end for my grand plan to teach high school.

In England we had the opportunity to watch and listen as John and Carol, Bob and Penny, Kenn and Joanie Gulliksen, Blaine and Becky Cook, and, of course, Lonnie Frisbee all prayed for healing, cast out demons, and saw people filled with the Spirit. Not only did we watch and listen but we prayed alongside them. They would watch and listen as we prayed. We learned and grew and caught it—the kingdom ministry bug. It really was more caught than taught, and once you began to see God move through you, you couldn't do anything else.

Throughout the trip we would debrief. Gathered in a hotel lobby or restaurant, John or Carol would ask us to share our experiences. These were the teachable moments. We would be encouraged, given further instruction, then sent back to work.

This was very much informally formal discipleship (or formally informal discipleship?). A number of dynamics were taking place at once. While we were learning and growing in our understanding of ministry, we were also "catching it." Through the hands-on opportunities presented to us, we also gained the heart for ministry. Not only were specific skills being passed on but also the motivation for ministry.

During those years my life was transformed. I began to grow in compassion, something I previously knew little about. I began to see people differently. Like Jesus in Matthew 9, I "saw" their plight, the pain they were in: harassed and often helpless, like sheep without a shepherd. And I began to feel something inside, to be moved by what I saw. But it didn't end there. I also began to realize that it wasn't enough to see the pain of others and feel compassion toward them and not act. I was compelled to do what Jesus did. To pray, and not only to pray but also to act. To do whatever I could to connect the pain in people's lives with the healing presence of Jesus. That can't be taught.

The rabbinic model of discipleship John subscribed to is based on the Jewish model of the disciple, or student, committing to the authority and leadership of the rabbi, or teacher. Unlike many contemporary models there is no set curriculum, agenda, or close-ended time frame. Rather, it is an ongoing relationship. It involves as much a transfer of essence as information. Another thing John said in the context of discipleship was, "Pour your essence into people. It's bigger than what you're training them for."

The student's life is closely observed by the teacher, and the teacher's life is observed by the student. The teacher will ask questions of the student: "Why did you do what you did?" "What did you learn?" "What might you do differently?" As the student processes, she or he also begins to emulate the teacher.

There is a responsibility placed on the teacher, but it is one that anyone wanting to make disciples will be willing to carry. If we aren't confident that our lives are an adequate reflection of what life in Christ looks like, we should consider taking a step back and furthering our own discipleship process first. This shouldn't necessarily cause someone to feel inadequate or shrink away from discipleship. We are all continually learning and growing. One of the mysteries and beauties of the kingdom is that we can be disciplers and disciples at the same time.

One of the values of this rabbinic model is that the ministry-related questions are the building blocks leading to real-life questions and conversation. The disciple and teacher develop a bond that may be for a season or, like that of Paul and Timothy, for many years. It may last a lifetime. Regardless of duration, the relationship is always of the moment. Teachers have the opportunity to pour their essence into students and transfer whatever they have from God to them. It behooves us to be mindful of this and make the most of every opportunity to pass on what we know and who we are.

I observed John on numerous occasions doing just that. With staff and leaders he had significant opportunity to pour into them. With others he may have had only a moment or two: a brief conversation at the end of a service or during a walk down the hallway. John would utilize every opportunity to encourage someone or remind them of their gifts. He had an amazing memory (or maybe it was the Holy Spirit—I can't be sure) when it came to reminding people of things they had done or said in the past that could encourage them. His actions were a tremendous example for me. I learned, or at least started to learn, the value of making the most of opportunities and speaking truth and life into the heart of another person.

# CHAPTER 8

# FAITH IS SPELLED
# R-I-S-K

*Then Peter got down out of the boat, walked
on the water and came toward Jesus.*
—MATTHEW 14:29

Faith is, without a doubt, risky business. "Faith is spelled R-I-S-K" is unquestionably one of John's most impactful statements. There are at least a couple of itinerant conference speakers active today who are making a living off this message alone. For many of us raised in the seventies, the teaching proliferated by the faith movement was a powerful influence. Christians were taught via television and radio that if they just have enough faith, God would do what they were asking. The most damaging impact of this was in the arena of healing. When someone wasn't healed, the onus was put on the person who was sick: "You must not have had enough faith." Those who were already suffering add guilt and the question "Where do I get more faith?" to their plight?

John spoke into this environment. "Faith is spelled R-I-S-K" is a two-edged sword. One side is an exhortation to take risks—to step out and do those kingdom things that we might feel led to do but just aren't sure about.

If we don't take a risk, we know the outcome. Nothing will happen. Nothing. If we do risk, the options multiply exponentially. Maybe, just maybe, God will heal the person or otherwise answer our prayer. Maybe they won't be healed on the spot but will feel loved and cared for. Maybe they won't accept prayer at all but will go away and think about the exchange. Maybe they'll go home and tell everyone they know about what happened and full-scale revival will break out. If we risk, we don't know what might happen; the options are limitless. It's frightening. Saving face and looking good is always a priority for me, and taking risks requires laying down not only the fear but a measure of self-indulgence.

The other edge of that sword is a healing ointment for anyone who has ever prayed for the sick or been prayed for and not healed. It's not your fault. It's not your lack of faith. Praying is a step of faith. When we pray, we are trusting God to hear, to respond. To not pray is a lack of faith, but every time we step out and ask God to heal, we are taking a risk and exercising faith. Faith is a commitment to move in a direction toward God. It is not being certain of the outcome. Anyone who is willing to take those fearful, little steps of faith should be commended, and no one who is sick or in pain should feel guilty over their pain. That's just not the kingdom of God.

Another dynamic of the faith equation is that we can risk and be used by God to convey healing to others even when we don't quite have it all together. This is true in the context of healing as well. John had numerous health issues throughout his life and was occasionally criticized for being overweight and unhealthy, but it never stopped him from praying for others. God will use us where we are today, especially if we are willing to rise above our circumstances, take that risk, and pray for others.

During the five days my daughter and her surrogate, Hollie, were in the hospital awaiting the birth of the twins, Jourdan and Hollie felt considerable apprehension, as you might imagine.[1] They dealt with it by playing worship music, praying, and reading Scripture together. God's presence was palpable in the room, and hospital staff began to notice.

One morning a nurse came in. "I heard something was going on in here. Can I talk to you guys for a minute?" She began to share her heart and confessed a long separation from God. A friend of hers, another nurse, had told her she should consider going back to church. Jourdan and Hollie prayed for her, and the Holy Spirit touched her deeply. In the midst of their own challenges, while not knowing what the outcome would be, they stepped out of their pain and as wounded healers brought life in Christ to another. A couple of days later the nurse's friend, who had heard what happened, came by to say thank you. She shared that she had a two-year-old daughter with a severe genetic defect, and they prayed for her.

Over the next several months, Hollie, Jourdan, and numerous other people from our church visited this woman's home and prayed with her, her husband, and their daughter, Lulu, on several occasions.

There is a risk anytime we step out in faith. John would say, "It's like jumping off of the diving board and trusting God to fill the pool before you land." I'm not sure it's quite that dramatic, but there is an element of risk even when we pray with those we know. But God is good to smooth the path and give us little signs of grace along the way.

# CHAPTER 9

## TEACH THE BIBLE, NOT YOUR EXPERIENCE

*Your word is a lamp for my feet,*
*a light on my path.*
—PSALM 119:105

One of John's most valuable lessons addressed the tendency to theologize, or justify from Scripture, an experience we had with the Lord so that others could have it as well. One problem with this is that God doesn't work that way. He created each person as a unique individual, and the way each of us experiences God is unique to our personality, our spirit, and our one-of-a-kind soul. Yet another problem is that our experience will always fall short of God's Word. We will never, in this lifetime, experience all that he has for us. Any attempt to theologize to reproduce our experience in others is to limit God, not walk in what God has.

If we want to experience all that God has for us, we will stay true to his Word and not succumb to the temptation to teach our experience. Many of us have heard John share his account of teaching on healing for a full year before anyone was healed. It was an interesting time in the life of Anaheim Vineyard. Week after week John would teach from the Gospels the various accounts of Jesus healing people. He would talk about the kingdom of God and how when we pray "your kingdom come, your will be done, on earth as it is in heaven" that we are, in fact, asking for just that. For God's rule to come and his will to be done here, now, in this person's body, just as it will one day be in heaven.

At the end of each service the ministry team would be dispatched, and people would respond to a call for prayer. And very little happened. Oh, people felt loved and cared for. We learned to pray and to listen to the voice of the Holy Spirit. As we listened to John and did further study in small groups, we grew in confidence that God's will was to heal people.

But no one got healed. It would be easy to give up in a situation like that. To just move on and teach something else. But John was convicted that Scripture taught healing, and he continued to teach healing. We in the church also pressed in and continued to pray and seek God for healing. That was the focus. But years later, as a pastor responsible for teaching Scripture to my own congregation, it was John's tenacity and devotion to the Word that spoke most loudly to me. I realized that no matter how difficult the lessons of Scripture were, I was obliged to teach them with no compromise and no shame.

As pastors and leaders, we are obliged to teach the truth of Scripture. This doesn't mean denying the difference between experience and truth or pretending our experience is something that it isn't, but instead just knowing that the truth has inherent power to transform those we speak to. A primary function of Christian leadership is to help those we influence to navigate life's challenges in the grace of God. To help them learn that the path to resurrection on Sunday is through crucifixion on Friday. To do this we must stay true to what Scripture teaches and avoid the temptation to soften it or mold it to fit our experiences or circumstances.

# CHAPTER 10

# PEOPLE WILL GO TO CHURCH FOR A LOT OF REASONS, BUT THEY'LL ONLY STAY FOR ONE— RELATIONSHIP

*And let us consider how we may spur one another on toward love and good deeds, not giving up meeting together, as some are in the habit of doing, but encouraging one another—and all the more as you see the Day approaching.*
—HEBREWS 10:24–25

In the early days of the Anaheim Vineyard, the answer to almost every question was, "You should go to a kinship group." For example, if you went up for prayer after a service, regardless of the outcome of the prayer or what it was you were asking prayer for, the ministry team person praying for you would very likely say, "If you'd like to get further ministry, the best place to do that would be at a kinship group." Likewise, if you were interested in learning more about spiritual gifts and how to incorporate them into the fabric of your faith, you would be directed to a kinship group and told that's where you could best learn more. And again, if someone new inquired about how to get more involved in the life of the church, they, too, would be directed to a kinship group.

"Kinship" was the name given to the home groups at Anaheim Vineyard. The name comes from the Old Testament book of Ruth and the concept of the kinsman-redeemer or nearest relative. It carries with it the concept of family and fellowship. Kinships were places where people could get to know others and be known by others. They were intentionally structured simply to be easily reproducible. The focus wasn't on Bible study, but on relationship. That's not to say Bible study was prohibited in any way, but the intent and focus was always on building lasting and mutually accountable relationships.

The format for a typical group meeting would begin with fellowship over coffee and dessert followed by worship with space left for the gifts of the spirit to be expressed and practiced. After that, there was a time of sharing. The conversation would be facilitated by a leader but not controlled or dominated by any one person. The intention was that every person would have equal opportunity to share.

After sharing, there would normally be prayer ministry. Sometimes the group would break down into even smaller groups of three or four to ensure that everyone had opportunity to receive prayer as well as pray for others. When a group reached twelve to fifteen people, the leaders would work with "apprentice" leaders and make plans to divide into two groups. This also maximized the potential for real relationships.

John's experience visiting hundreds of churches while working for Fuller Seminary gave him an acute awareness of the importance of relationship. He understood that not even the best worship team, the most dynamic preacher, or the most exciting children's ministry could keep people around if they didn't connect. He was very aware of the inherent need in every person to know and be known.

He also believed that the church was the best vehicle for relationships to be developed. While other clubs or groups might have a semblance of relationship, they lacked the depth and authenticity brought by the presence of the Holy Spirit. Essentially, a focused and intentional group of people combined with the presence of God creates a powerful recipe for deep relationship. This was my experience and Donna's as well. We both began attending kinship groups early in our time at Anaheim and found them a place of acceptance and warmth. In the context of these groups, I really learned how to be a Christian—and a responsible adult for that matter.

In the context of kinship, we learned about the things of the Spirit and how to live life in the presence of the Spirit. We learned that it's a spiritual thing to go to work every day and pay your bills on time. We saw what it looked like to be married and raise kids. To make good decisions and "grow up before we grew old."

Our groups during those years were not segregated by age or any other demographic distinction. Donna was in her early teens and came from a non-Christian background. The group we attended was composed of singles and married couples, young and old. The diversity was refreshing. I don't recall ever feeling out of place or in any way on the outside. We learned about life from a biblical perspective, with or without the proof texts. Some of the relationships we developed in those groups have been with us ever since. When we were married in 1982, the four-year-old daughter of our group's leaders was our flower girl. In 2010, she called and asked me to officiate her wedding.

Anaheim was a large church at that time, with three to four thousand people in attendance on Sunday. But the people you sat with and related to were the people you went to kinship with. Those ten or twelve were, effectively, your church. The other three thousand just provided a meaningful atmosphere for a worship experience. It never actually happened, but I always thought it would be telling if each group wore a different-colored T-shirt to the service. You would see all red in one section, blue in another, yellow in another. Kinship groups were the bedrock of relationship that enabled people to feel connected and have a sense of belonging and ownership in a large church.

Of course, relationship is not simply a Vineyard Value or a clever church-growth mechanism; it is a core human need. We are created in the image of God, who is intrinsically relational. His deepest desire is to have relationship with his creation. God saw all he had made as very good, but he also said it wasn't good for the man to be alone. Our longing for relationship was strategically placed by God. It's clear throughout Scripture that connection with others is vital to our spiritual, emotional, and mental well-being. Consider the "one another" passages scattered throughout Paul's epistles. It goes without saying that none of those things could happen in isolation.

Curiously, for someone known for his supernatural healing ministry, John believed that even healing happens in the context of relationship. He was committed to a much more holistic approach to healing than many people realized. If you attended a conference or visited a Sunday night service at Anaheim Vineyard, you might witness John giving a few words of knowledge related to healing. He would then ask if the words related to anyone present and, if so, would have people pray for those who responded. This was the public image of healing that was seen by those outside the church. However, if Anaheim was your home church, you would also experience the healing that took place week by week, as a committed group of friends would pray for you, walk through difficult times with you, and support you even when you were in sin or out of sorts in some capacity.

Yet another powerful dynamic associated with relationship and healing that John understood is that every person has a vital contribution to make. Not only do we have an inherent need to belong, but we also need to make a valuable contribution—that is, to be needed. Relationship is a two-way street. We need to know and be known. To love and be loved. The purpose and value that come with contributing have a profound impact on our spiritual growth. Again, this can be found only in relationship.

The discovery of one's spiritual gifts is a vital component in discipleship. The very nature of spiritual gifts requires relationship. The gifts are given by God, to be used by us to touch others.

In the context of relationship, we discover our gifts, grow in them, and learn to use them effectively. As we learn to confidently yet humbly minister, our identity in Christ is formed and we move toward wholeness.

CHAPTER 11

# THE WAY IN IS
# THE WAY ON

*So then, just as you received Christ Jesus*
*as Lord, continue to live your lives in him.*
—COLOSSIANS 2:6

John captured an essential spiritual truth in his pithy little saying, "The way in is the way on." He was deeply committed to an ongoing relationship with Christ earmarked by (1) intimacy cultivated in worship and prayer, (2) understanding cultivated in study of the Scripture, (3) character cultivated in service, and (4) community cultivated in fellowship. One of the most valuable lessons I learned from John was that Christianity is a process, not an event.

We tend to base our faith on events: the next conference, the next retreat, the next worship gathering. John understood that those are part of our spiritual journey and needed in the process of our growth. The danger comes when those events are the full expression of our growth. He called them "power points" and valued them—he even wrote a book about them. However, his focus was always on walking out our faith in the context of everyday life where it is lived—at work, at school, at home, in the marketplace.

I received Christ by faith. I took a step of faith and made a commitment to accept and follow him. This happened in the context of relationship. I was attending a youth group at a local denominational church my freshman year in high school. I enjoyed the group; both the other youth and the leaders were accepting and friendly. I had been attending for several months when it was announced that we were going on an outing that weekend. There was a movie playing at the Fox Fullerton Theatre called *A Thief in the Night*. I joined the group and went to the show. I don't remember anything about the movie, but I do remember what happened next.

As the movie ended the lights came on, and a man walked out in front of the screen and started talking. Weird. I'd never seen anything like that before. I listened and at some point realized that I believed everything he was saying, but I had never done what he was saying I needed to do. At the end of his speech the man invited anyone who wanted to accept Jesus to come forward and make a commitment. It seemed like the right thing to do. I didn't feel any strong leading or inspiration. It just kind of made sense, so I went for it.

That's how I came to Christ. I decided that day to step forward and follow Jesus. I have tried every day in the forty-six years since to do the same thing. Get up in the morning and decide to follow Jesus. The way in is the way on. It isn't always easy, and, I'll be honest, there have been more than a few days when, despite my decision, I didn't follow very well. The beauty, I suppose, is that I can get up again tomorrow and make that decision *one more time*. Growing up under John's leadership taught me that I just needed to keep going regardless of what was happening around me or how I felt at the moment.

There were people in our church who would go forward for prayer every week. One woman in particular would go up front week after week, often crying, and receive prayer. At first I thought, *Is that lady ever gonna get better?* But as time went on, I realized she had it figured out. She knew she needed to go to Jesus again, and again, and again. She knew he would meet her there, and that he never tired of her coming to him for more. The way in is the way on.

What is the way in? Grace is the way in. When we come to Jesus his arms are open, his heart receives us, and he sets another place at the table. Regardless of where we've come from, prodigal daughters and sons all, he says, "Welcome home."

In the early nineties I was leading a young adult service at the Anaheim Vineyard called the eight o'clock service. It was a midweek meeting at, you guessed it, 8:00 p.m. The attendees were largely an alternative crowd: musicians, artists, and various and sundry (to borrow another Wimberism) other bohemians. Many who came were churched and simply enjoyed a more cultural expression of worship, but many were not. They had been invited by coworkers or roommates, and this midweek service was their church. One evening, at the end of the service, a young woman came forward for prayer. She was probably in her mid to late twenties but had a hardened face that made her look older. She was crying, and her mascara had run down her cheeks, adding to an overall hot-mess effect. I sat down on the stage steps next to her, along with a couple of gals from our ministry team.

"How's it going?" I asked.

"I haven't been to church since Easter when I was twelve, and—and . . . and those songs." Her heart had been touched during worship by the grace of God. She had found a God who didn't judge her or expect her to clean up her act first; he just welcomed her home.

It's easy as we continue our journeys to lose sight of that. To try supplementing growth with things of our own making. Disciplines, rules, structures. All are good and necessary but only when done in the context of grace. When we lose sight of grace, our best efforts become rote and our faith becomes brittle. I find I need to rediscover the Jesus that young lady discovered on a regular basis.

I also witnessed this long obedience in John's life. John put on conferences and spoke at events all over the world, but he was first a churchman. He was fiercely devoted to the local church. His travel was often midweek, and even after arriving home on a Friday or Saturday jet-lagged and tired, he would speak on Sunday. The majority of the congregation likely didn't even know he'd been gone.

John was at church regularly, even through the series of illnesses he endured in the nineties. Very early on he used to preach just sitting behind his Fender Rhodes. After worship he would take the offering and simply open his Bible and preach. Later he became a little more conventional and stood behind a pulpit like a normal preacher, but in the nineties he sat on a stool, weakened from chemotherapy and needing stability.

But he still preached. John often said that when we accept Jesus, we accept his church and his cause as well; the three are inseparable, and you can't have one without the others. For John, being engaged in a grace-filled community was the way in and the way on.

# CHAPTER 12

# I'M JUST A FAT MAN ON
# MY WAY TO HEAVEN

*Be completely humble and gentle; be*
*patient, bearing with one another in love.*
—EPHESIANS 4:2

When my children were young, I would often read to them at night. In 1993 *The Book of Virtues* by William Bennett was published. It contains great moral stories that I enjoyed reading to the kids. Bennett covers the virtues of self-discipline, compassion, responsibility, friendship, work, courage, perseverance, honesty, loyalty, and faith. While the book is a beautiful collection of stories conveying lessons of truth and integrity, one virtue is conspicuously missing—humility. The lost virtue. Humility isn't as honored in our culture today as it has been in the past—certainly not to the degree it is in Scripture. Jesus, Paul, Peter, and James all exhort their readers to be humble.

John Wimber was also a leader who valued humility. He told me once that "humility is a clear understanding of where you end and God begins." John helped me understand how humility works. It's taking an honest evaluation of what I have accomplished and then asking myself this question: *What could I have accomplished without God's guidance, provision, wisdom, grace, and leading?* Well, the answer is "nothing." Beginning with every breath I take, I can do nothing without him. This perspective will foster humility.

No statement describes John's value for being humble and naturally supernatural more than "I'm just a fat man on my way to heaven." To be naturally supernatural, as John defined it, was to enact the supernatural ministry of Jesus in and through our own lives, while being who we really are as human beings. Doing so with no pretense, no show, no big voice or big words, just naturally. John was not impressed by fame or celebrity status, including his own. He used self-deprecating humor to make the point that we are all simple servants of Jesus, and that Jesus is the one who deserves the glory for any ministry success he allows us to participate in.

The beauty of being naturally supernatural is that it takes some of the mystique out of being used by God. Sometimes, when we see a gifted person up on stage moving in the power of the Spirit or speaking eloquently, our automatic response is, "That's great for them, but I could never do that." John's manner and approach disarmed those objections and made it possible for hundreds, even thousands, of people to feel confident stepping out in kingdom ministry. "If a fat guy in a Hawaiian shirt can do this, maybe I can too."

Another value communicated by this Wimberism is that there are no superstars. Not only can anybody do this, but everybody's contribution is equally valuable. The ethos surrounding the Anaheim Vineyard during John's tenure was very much one of a freedom to risk and to fall short. Any ministry outing that didn't go as planned was viewed as an educational experience rather than an outright failure. What did you learn? What will you do differently? Great, go again!

John maintained that humility was the primary component in effective biblical leadership. He wrote: "Unlike the managerial or professional models of leadership, the key is not mastering certain skills or accumulating knowledge. The key is humility—humble character and humble dependence on the Lord."[1]

When John said, "I'm just a fat man on my way to heaven," he erased the clergy versus laity distinction. He was saying in effect, "I'm just like you." Oh, maybe you're a slender woman on her way to heaven, or a short, prematurely balding dude on his way to heaven, but we're all the same. We're all equally flawed and equally loved by God. We're all of inestimable worth to him. And we all have a contribution to make to his kingdom. Believing that about ourselves has the power to keep us humble.

# CHAPTER 13

# BORROW FROM TOMORROW

*Give us today our daily bread.*
—MATTHEW 6:11

*The Lord is my shepherd, I lack nothing.*
—PSALM 23:1

"Borrow from tomorrow" was John's paraphrase of the petition in the Lord's prayer that we typically read as "Give us today our daily bread." The Greek word translated *daily* is *epiousios*, and it literally means "the approaching day" or "coming day." John understood and taught that this prayer is not a simple request for godly provision but a kingdom request for the provision that we will one day know in heaven—today! It's a prayer to bring the kingdom to bear on hunger, poverty, homelessness, and injustice. It's a cry for God to release his kingdom rule on all that is lacking in the world and to release his people into a place of kingdom provision.

This phrase is a continuation of the one that precedes it: "Your kingdom come, your will be done, on earth as it is in heaven" (v. 10). We are asking for the reign of God, which we will know and enjoy with him in the future, to be active and present in our current situation. We see this reign in healing and freedom from oppression. We see it when justice disrupts the injustices of human trafficking or racial discrimination. To pray "give us today our daily bread" is to ask for that same kingdom dynamic in the realm of poverty and provision.

Jesus' ministry was one of words and works, prayer and action. We are called to both as well. It's my conviction that social action without kingdom power is incomplete, and that prayer without action is a hollow gesture.[1] Not long ago I was volunteering at our church's food pantry, King's Kindness. My job that particular Thursday was to walk people out to their cars, pushing their shopping carts for them. This is my favorite job. The pantry is typically busy and loud, but that one- or two-minute journey to the car provides opportunity for one-on-one interaction.

I was walking out with a Middle Eastern man named Sal. I asked, "How's it going, Sal?" He responded that he was very down and not sure what to do next. He had been working in the States for seven years, but his wife was still in their home country of Syria. Sal was here legally, and they had filed every petition and done all they knew to do to bring her here to join him, but to no avail.

Sal was brokenhearted. The groceries in the basket seemed a small consolation to his pain. I had no real answers and felt somewhat helpless, but I said, "I'm sorry, Sal. I'll pray for you."

When I said that, he began sobbing. He looked at me and said, "You're the first person who has ever said they would pray for me." I was standing in a parking lot in Tigard, Oregon, in 2016, with a forty-five-year-old man whom no one had ever prayed for. I began to cry as well. I put my arms around him and prayed the only prayer I could think of: "Let your kingdom come and your will be done, on earth as it is in heaven. Give Sal the provision you will have for him in heaven, right here, right now."

When we place ourselves in position to do the natural things, we just might see God do supernatural things. Caring for the poor is ingrained in the DNA of the Vineyard Movement. It is as much a part of who God has called us to be as is worship or healing. It was John's heart from the onset that the Vineyard would consist of people who lean toward the poor. He wrote: "As we get healthy as a [church] body, it becomes of major importance that we reach out to the oppressed poor. We must not miss our commission to minister to them. It is an expression of our health and understanding of what God has done for us."[2]

John firmly believed that ministry to those in need was a primary intersection of the natural and supernatural. Many people who are impoverished financially are also suffering physically, emotionally, and mentally, and when we open the doors to provide for physical needs, we create a platform for prayer and an opportunity to meet spiritual needs as well.

# CHAPTER 14

# DON'T LET ANYONE ELSE IN FOR LESS THAN WHAT YOU PAID

*Whoever can be trusted with very little can also be trusted with much, and whoever is dishonest with very little will also be dishonest with much.*
—LUKE 16:10

Are leaders born or are they made? This age-old question has been pondered and debated for millennia. John understood that the best answer was "both/and." Some individuals seem to be natural-born leaders. They inevitably end up in leadership despite their best efforts to skirt those positions. In *The Making of a Leader*, Bobby Clinton calls this "sovereign foundations."[1] Clinton, along with J. Oswald Sanders and others, recognizes true leadership as a gift from God.[2]

Like John, those authors recognize that leadership is a responsibility that must be taken seriously and developed by co-operating with God while becoming the leader he has appointed one to be. Leaders are not only born but also made; there are clearly traits that can be developed and honed to make someone a more effective leader.

One of the last things John said to me as I was preparing to leave for Portland to plant a church was "Don't let anyone else in for less than you paid." I knew what he meant. My path into ministry hadn't always been easy. I owned a small but successful gardening business prior to going on staff at Anaheim, and when I transitioned, I took a significant cut in pay.

My responsibilities at Anaheim Vineyard included being both the youth pastor and the janitor. Often those responsibilities overlapped. Our youth program ran on Sunday morning during the main service. That was also the time of the week when the most people were in the building at the same time. On many occasions I had to leave the youth in the hands of my volunteer staff while I ran off to fill empty toilet-paper holders or, worse, unplug a clogged toilet. Then I went right back to teaching the youth about patience or faithfulness or some other relevant topic.

I can't honestly say that I always appreciated those times. But they were an excellent preparation for a life in ministry. Learning to serve, and not on my own terms or in my own time, helped prepare me for what I would be doing the rest of my life. Crises— whether a tragic accident, diagnosis of cancer or another terminal illness, or any number of other life events that a pastor might be called to respond to—don't happen on our terms. Those things never come when it's convenient. They inevitably happen at the least opportune times. And, like me, you may have discovered that they never happen one at a time. When a crisis hits the life of someone in our church, it's usually accompanied by one or two others. (Can I get an "Amen"?)

John was committed to developing young leaders. He understood that leadership isn't formed in a vacuum but, like so much of the Christian life, happens in relationship. Specifically, the relationship of a mentor or leader to a young apprentice. He also believed in releasing commensurate degrees of authority and responsibility at appropriate times and functioning as a pacesetter in a young leader's development, recognizing that humble and less prominent tasks were indicators of how a prospective leader would handle greater levels of authority and responsibility. It's imperative that a senior leader not hold back an aspiring leader and squelch passion, instead giving just enough at the right time to allow the protégé to mature, while developing discernment and character in their own right.

Eventually, I "graduated" and my janitorial responsibilities were replaced with other levels of pastoral authority. This transition process seemed laboriously long to me at the time, but I realize now that God—and a good mentor—will always advance us more slowly than we would like. Time and again in the Psalms, David bemoans, "How long, O Lord, how long?"

Character development doesn't happen overnight. Mature leadership isn't formed overnight. The process, while slow, is also invaluable. Leadership requires the ability to assess situations and take time to process decisions. John understood this well and released responsibility appropriately.

Why did John tell me not to let anyone else in for less than I paid? Because he was also committed to spiritual reproduction. He wasn't interested in just releasing leaders but in releasing leaders who would in turn release other leaders. Like Paul's admonition to Timothy: "And the things you have heard me say in the presence of many witnesses entrust to reliable people who will also be qualified to teach others."[3] John was mentoring me to mentor others. He knew I was going to plant a church, and he desired it to be a reproducing church and for me to be a reproducing leader. He was both encouraging me and challenging me not to be too easy on those whom I would train and release, giving them the same quality of training I had received.

This wasn't an easy lesson to learn. I confess that at times I let others "in for less than I paid." I've been reluctant to ask aspiring young leaders to do some of the mundane things I did. That's proved to be a mistake. Inevitably, too much too soon will "spoil them," as Sanders says.[4] Ultimately, I as a mentor do them a disservice by not helping instill the quality of character that is built through learning to serve and being available to help in whatever capacity is required. Serving in those less glamorous roles helps young leaders see the big picture and gain an appreciation for what it takes to effectively run a church or ministry. I learned the importance of clean restrooms. I want the leaders whom I have the opportunity to sow into to learn those lessons as well, and to become the very best and most compassionate leaders they can be.

# CHAPTER 15

# THE VIEW FROM THE VALLEY AIN'T THAT BAD

*Blessed are those whose strength is in you,*
*whose hearts are set on pilgrimage.*
*As they pass through the Valley of Baka,*
*they make it a place of springs;*
*the autumn rains also cover it with pools.*
*They go from strength to strength,*
*till each appears before God in Zion.*
    —PSALM 84:5–7

*God whispers to us in our pleasures, speaks*
*in our consciences, but shouts in our pain.*
*It is his megaphone to rouse a deaf world.*
    —C. S. LEWIS

John was somewhat unusual in his time (although less so today) in that, while being best known for a healing ministry, he also embraced a theology of suffering. He understood that one of the tensions of the kingdom of God is that while we pray, "Let your kingdom come and your will be done, on earth as it is in heaven," this won't always be reality in our lives. The nature of the kingdom in this age and the reality of spiritual warfare dictate that occasionally our Enemy will win a battle. Sickness, sin, death, and suffering will all be faced in this lifetime.

He also understood that our character will be refined through suffering, and we will become more and more Christlike in the process. John wrote: "The goal of the Christian life is maturity in Christ, to become like Jesus. But how are we to attain this high goal? In our own strength it is impossible. But Jesus can accomplish it in us, and one of the means he uses to gain his lofty goal is obedience in suffering."[1]

John not only embraced a theology of suffering; he humbly and transparently lived that theology out. While not pointing to illness as a primary vehicle for suffering (John saw persecution as the primary means by which Christians suffer but also included sickness, temptation, and the pain caused by loss and the negative circumstances of life), he was aware that anyone in physical pain was suffering, especially those with a chronic condition. And while he passionately prayed for healing, he also challenged his congregation to recognize that pain was yet another means by which God could refine their lives.

I have a vivid memory of a particular Sunday evening service. John had only recently returned to preaching after treatment for cancer (it may have been his first week back; I can't remember), and he was talking about how we, as people, love mountaintop experiences. But, he cautioned, life isn't lived on the mountain-top. Then he paused and said, "Besides, I've been in the valley, and the view from the valley ain't that bad."

It struck me that God could take the pain in our lives and use it to make us better people. We can become bitter or better. He will shape and form us into the image of Christ if we allow him to. He will cause patience, empathy, grace, and forgiveness to grow in our hearts and then use us to bring comfort to others who are suffering.

But that can only happen if we are willing to walk through the valley—the valley of Baka, the valley of the shadow, whatever valley life leads us into. Not only will God use those difficult times to extract growth in our lives; he will also speak to us in the midst of them.

C. S. Lewis wrote: "God whispers to us in our pleasures, speaks in our consciences, but shouts in our pain. It is his mega-phone to rouse a deaf world."[2] The most challenging times in our lives are often when we most clearly hear the voice of the Lord. When all is well, on the mountaintop so to speak, our natural tendency is to put life on autopilot and enjoy the ride. In the valley we are aware of our need for the Lord, we pray more diligently, and we listen more acutely.

John also maintained that going through trials and challenges would deepen our sense of God's presence. He wrote: "We want to engender a deep spirituality in our disciples that rejects a facile triumphalism. Disciples realize that there will be hard times ahead. The journey we're on is fraught with pain, difficulties and the onslaughts of the Enemy. They also learn we can benefit from trials."[3]

He was not fatalistic and would not give up praying for someone who was ill or in a difficult situation. He was simply aware that we have an Enemy and live in a fallen world. John walked, and taught his church to walk, in the tension of "the now and the not yet," avowing that the kingdom is here and now. He taught us to pray, "Let your kingdom come here, today, into this situation, and let your will be done right now, in this person's life." We prayed while remaining acutely aware that our job was to pray in obedience, but the responsibility to bring change lay firmly with the Lord.

The influence of the George Eldon Ladd's teaching on John is well documented. John embraced Ladd's kingdom theology and put it into practice to an extent not previously done. In *The Gospel of the Kingdom*, Ladd wrote: "We shall never experience the full blessings of God's kingdom in this Age. There are those who have identified the Christian hope with a warless world or with a world completely subdued to God's will through the preaching of the gospel. People who fix their hopes upon a kingdom which is to be consummated in this age are certain to be disillusioned. The perfected kingdom belongs to the age to come."[4] John taught this reality and put it into practice at Anaheim and in the conferences and seminars he conducted. He was unwilling to give people a triumphalist view that was pastorally untenable.

I am grateful for this perspective. I have walked through profoundly painful times with people and have found the tension of the kingdom and the dynamic of spiritual warfare to be a much more pastorally sensitive and biblically sound response than "You just didn't have enough faith." I then help folks process what is happening in their lives in a more productive way, encouraging them to press into the Lord and allow the God of all comfort to breathe new life into their sorrow.[5]

# CHAPTER 16

## DIAL DOWN

*After the earthquake came a fire, but the*
*Lord was not in the fire. And after the fire*
*came a gentle whisper.*
—1 KINGS 19:12

During one of the conferences held at Anaheim in the mid-eighties, I was part of the ministry team praying with people who responded to John's direction for ministry. On this occasion it was getting late, and ministry was beginning to wind down. People were connecting with their friends and heading out for coffee and dessert or back to their hotels.

There were still a few folks waiting for prayer. I approached a woman who had a fearful look on her face. I asked what I could pray for, and she launched into a well-rehearsed discourse of the abuses she had endured, followed by symptoms: "nightmares, panic attacks, bouts of agoraphobia," and a list of the diagnoses she had received from doctors, counselors, and therapists: "schizophrenia, bipolar, dissociative identity disorder," and on and on. It was almost as though someone had pushed the play button and she was simply repeating information she had given many times before.

I was tired and admittedly overwhelmed. Where was I to begin? I felt compassion for her. She had obviously come in desperation, looking for help. I was reminded of the woman who had been bleeding for twelve years and reached out to touch the edge of Jesus' robe. In a moment of Holy Spirit–inspired wisdom, I asked her, "What would you like Jesus to do for you right now?"

My question caught her off guard. She thought for a moment before replying, "If the noise in my head would just stop."

I smiled and said, "Let's pray for that." I asked the Holy Spirit to come and minister to her and then softly prayed that Jesus would quiet the noise in her head. I could see the peace of God rest on her and replace the fear I'd seen at first. After a few minutes, tears began to run down her cheeks (and mine). When we finished she said, "Thank you. It's quiet now."

One of the little phrases John used often when teaching people to pray for healing was "dial down." As short and sweet as it is, it's also fraught with meaning. Dial down meant to take a spiritual step back—to wait. To listen. To approach the situation calmly and in the presence of God. It meant to resist the temptation to let our own emotions take control of a situation but rather focus all our attention on the Lord and what he was doing at the moment. Dial down also meant to pray in a naturally supernatural way, in our own voice, with no increased volume or religious language. John would say, "God isn't hard-of-hearing and doesn't speak exclusively in King James English."

Dial down was also an encouragement not to emulate anyone else in prayer—to be ourselves. The person God would use in this situation, at this time, in this place was me, not Benny Hinn or Oral Roberts, not John Wimber, but me. Each person trained to minister was encouraged to pray in a manner that was comfortable and genuine for them rather than follow a predetermined formula. While we learned the five-step healing model, we were often reminded that it was just that—a model. The simple steps could be followed while being authentic in our prayers.

Overall, dial down was a philosophy of ministry. As a Wimberism, it articulated that the presence and power of the Holy Spirit could be accessed and released in ministry without the trappings of classic Pentecostalism. John modeled this in his own ministry style. While he's been called "folksy" and "laidback," those characteristics were intentional. Whether giving a word of knowledge, praying for healing, or casting out demons, John would remain calm and confident in the Spirit rather than boisterous or loud. He modeled an approach that was easily transferable and reproducible and that encouraged individuals to be authentic.

Dialing down also involves listening. It means we leave space in our prayer for the Holy Spirit to speak. Culturally, we're conditioned to expect immediate results and to "get the job done." The approach John presented was one of patience, one of waiting, and one of listening.

Waiting on the Spirit was a carryover from John's Quaker days. In his book *A People Called Quakers*, Elton Trueblood quoted a Quaker founder: "And while waiting upon the Lord in silence, as often we did for many hours together, we received often the pouring down of the Spirit upon us."[1] John taught us to be patient, to listen, to wait, and to cultivate the ability to hear from the Holy Spirit.

# CHAPTER 17

# BELIEVE YOUR BELIEFS AND DOUBT YOUR DOUBTS

*I do believe; help me overcome my unbelief!*
—MARK 9:24

*But when you ask, you must believe and not doubt.*
—JAMES 1:6

On our first England trip, in the summer of 1981 (the one I was supernaturally conscripted into going on), I had a "believe your beliefs and doubt your doubts" moment. It was only the second or third night, and I had convinced myself that I was not qualified to be on the team. I was certain that I was the very worst of all sinners, that God could and would use anyone *except* me, and that if I prayed for someone, they would undoubtedly get sicker or possibly die.

So I did what any red-blooded American child of God would do. I hid. St. Andrews Chorleywood had a kitchen off of the sanctuary, and as soon as John began the ministry time, I snuck through the door and sat down on an inverted five gallon bucket. I was only a couple of minutes into my self-imposed exile, when who should walk into the kitchen but Mr. Wimber himself. He walked over and gave me a look—a kind of all-knowing look—and asked, "What are you doing?"

"Hiding."

"Well, I didn't bring you here to hide, so get in there and pray for someone."

Reluctantly, and under compulsion, I went back into the sanctuary to pray. I found my friend Danny and went with him. I thought that at least if one of us was legit, anyone we prayed for might not die. We soon engaged with a middle-aged man who explained that he was a machinist. His hand had been caught in a machine and was permanently twisted into a half-closed fist. The palm of his hand was covered with gnarly scar tissue from the accident. He explained that working with machines was all he knew how to do, and that it required both hands. Both his physical condition and his livelihood had been affected. Not long after we began to pray, he started to slowly flex his hand open and closed. As we continued, the movements grew greater until he was opening and closing his hand freely. Not only did he regain full movement, but the scar tissue that was partially responsible for the lack of movement had disappeared. To my knowledge, he was completely healed.

John often said, "Believe your beliefs and doubt your doubts." What he was communicating was that our beliefs in Jesus—who he is, who he says we are, and what the Bible says about our identity and authority in Christ—are true and what the Enemy says about those things is, well, a lie. This little phrase has application beyond ministry situations and realistically is most applicable in the realm of our thinking and identity.

Let's be honest: we all are prone to wrestle with the idea that "I'm not good enough," or "God can forgive anyone of anything, except me." Those doubts will creep into our thinking and worm their way down from our minds into our hearts and spirits and begin to cripple us. Altogether too many of us are inflicted with pain caused by things spoken over us by influential people—parents, teachers, pastors—and are locked into those patterns of rejection and "belief" of those lies.

I had a friend who would physically cringe and get a pained expression on his face every time someone said the word *stupid*. His reaction was the result of being called stupid by his father throughout his childhood. While this friend, I'll call him Joe, was not the most academic person and didn't always do well in classroom settings, he was one of those mechanically inclined people who could look at something, take it apart, and put it back together again with no manual or cheat sheet. He could fix virtually anything and spent a considerable amount of his young adulthood repairing friends' cars.

Joe also had a heart of gold. He loved the Lord and loved others profoundly and, despite his own upbringing, never said an unkind word about anyone and never directed any ire or negative commentary toward other people. But at times he doubted his beliefs. Joe knew that he was a smart person. He also knew that he was of inestimable value to Jesus and that nothing, not a higher IQ or better grades or any other measure of human achievement, would cause God to love him any more than he did right now. But he still cringed when he heard the word *stupid*. At those moments his doubts overcame his beliefs.

Biblically, doubt is a bad thing. Jesus repeatedly instructed his followers and friends not to doubt, and James told us that for our prayers to be effective we must believe and not doubt. And yet how often is the course of our lives directed by doubt? I don't know how many people I've talked with over the years who, like my friend Joe, have been sucked into the vortex of demonic doubt and just haven't been able to live in the truth of what God says about them.

Doubt isn't a sin in and of itself, but it is the enemy of faith. Doubt is universal. All believers will experience it at times. We will all encounter those moments or seasons when God doesn't meet our expectations. Peter did. Thomas became famous for it.

Possibly no contemporary of Jesus expressed his doubt more honestly than John the Baptist, though. Languishing in Herod's prison cell, John began to doubt. He realized he might die there. He began to wonder why Jesus hadn't done anything to help. John was helping others, yet here he was locked in this dungeon.

So he sent friends to ask Jesus, "Are you the one who is to come, or should we expect someone else?" (Matt. 11:3). If anyone knew that Jesus was who he said he was, it should have been John. Certainly, he had heard his mother, Elizabeth, and Aunt Mary sharing stories of when they were pregnant and how the Holy Spirit spoke to them about who Jesus was and what was to come. John led the way, proclaiming, "Prepare the way for the Lord." John baptized Jesus. He saw the Holy Spirit rest on him and heard the Father say, "This is my Son, whom I love; with him I am well pleased" (Matt. 3:17). And yet now his own experience caused him to wonder, to doubt: "Is he the one? Did I miss it? Did I get it wrong?"

There will be times like these in our lives, when our unmet expectations will cause us to question. In those times it's imperative to know what we believe and to believe what we know. Jesus' response to John was: "Go back and report to John what you hear and see: The blind receive sight, the lame walk, those who have leprosy are cleansed, the deaf hear, the dead are raised, and the good news is proclaimed to the poor" (Matt. 11:4–5).

When doubt begins to grip our hearts and squeeze our belief, it's good to review how Jesus has been faithful to us in the past: the times he's healed us, cared for us, provided for us, and freed us from bondage. I find it helpful to recite back to God what he's done for me. Psalm 77 reminds us to "remember" what the Lord has done.

> "Will the Lord reject forever?
> Will he never show his favor again?
> Has his unfailing love vanished forever?
> Has his promise failed for all time?
> Has God forgotten to be merciful?
> Has he in anger withheld his compassion?"

> Then I thought, "To this I will appeal:
> the years when the Most High stretched out his
> right hand.

I will remember the deeds of the LORD;

> yes, I will remember your miracles of long ago.

I will consider all your works

> and meditate on all your mighty deeds."

Your ways, God, are holy.

> What god is as great as our God?

You are the God who performs miracles;

> you display your power among the peoples.

With your mighty arm you redeemed your people,

> the descendants of Jacob and Joseph.

(PS. 77:7–15)

*Remember* is a powerful word in Scripture. It's also a key to overcoming doubt. Remember. When we celebrate the Lord's Supper, we read Paul's admonition as passed on from Jesus: "Do this in remembrance of me" (1 Cor. 11:24–25). To remember what God has done will help free us from doubt and help us move forward in a more kingdom-focused mind-set.

# CHAPTER 18

# SHOW ME YOUR PUPPIES, AND I'LL GIVE YOU YOUR PAPERS

*By their fruit you will recognize them.*
*—MATTHEW 7:16*

John was a firm believer in functional leadership over positional leadership. We have all known those with a position or title that they are quite proud of, but who aren't functionally influencing people for the kingdom. There were a number of ways John expressed this. One of the best known was "Show me your puppies, and I'll give you your papers."

Another saying I'm sure he adopted from elsewhere, because I've heard it used in other contexts: "The proof is in the pudding."

Another was simply, "The easiest way to know if you're a leader is just to turn around and see if anyone is following you." All these are ways of communicating that if someone is truly called to a ministry, there will be fruit. Getting an education or having a desire aren't necessarily clear indicators of calling. Desire is one indicator, and getting an education is part of the preparation to walk out a calling, but John believed that neither is definitive. Jesus told us that fruit is the clearest expression of calling. This is true at any level of ministry, whether as a small group leader, children's ministry teacher, or pastor of a megachurch.

John was not inclined to "give someone their papers" if they didn't have a proven track record. If someone wanted to plant a church, he wanted to see them start, lead, and reproduce small groups first. This, philosophically, is the inverse of how pastoral ministry was often approached at that time. If a young man or woman went to seminary and got a degree, they were then presented with a "call" to a church in need of a pastor.

As a church planting movement, Vineyard was (and still is) somewhat more entrepreneurial. The implications of this are, first, starting new churches is much more commonplace than stepping into existing churches; and second, that a specific skill set is more important than a degree, as in starting a business. This is consistent with John's "caught more than taught" philosophy and the rabbinic model of training. Pastors and church planters were trained by tagging along with those who were already doing it. They would observe, ask questions, and learn on the job. They would then be given limited responsibility followed by feedback and ultimately freedom to try on their own.

This was my experience when I became the youth pastor. I was invited by Dale Temple, one of the associate pastors at the time, to help him start a youth group. There wasn't a youth ministry in the first few years of the church because the whole church was young. When it started in 1977, the average age of attendees was nineteen (which happened to be my age at the time), so the idea of a youth ministry seemed a bit ludicrous.

In fact, John liked to tell a story about a woman who came for the first time and approached him after the service. She noticed in the bulletin that there was no mention of any youth group and asked John when he was going to start one. He responded, "My whole church is a youth group!" But within a few years, as the church grew and settled into a more permanent location on Cerritos Boulevard in Anaheim, the congregation also grew with families, and the need for a youth program presented itself. Dale asked me to help get things going, and I agreed.

The youth group met on Sunday morning during the main service because we were a commuter church—some people driving thirty-five to forty minutes to attend—and the best opportunity to gather young people was when their parents were already going to be there. From the get-go we had a group of thirty kids. The challenge was getting them to form a community.

Most didn't know each other because their families drove from different locations. It was more of an unruly gang than a group. I observed as Dale led them in crowd-breakers and other activities designed to foster relationship. We planned monthly outings, and soon Dale asked me to begin making the announcements during the Sunday meeting.

Before long I was leading the crowd-breakers, planning and leading the monthly outings, and becoming the face of the group. Dale gradually released more and more ministry to me and observed how the group responded to me. It soon became clear that Dale's plan all along had been for me to lead the group. After a few months of watching me lead and training me how to recruit other leaders, it was all mine. This was an invaluable process that I have endeavored to duplicate.

I will often invite a young leader to tag along as I "do ministry," whether it's a hospital visit, teaching assignment, or outreach. I invite them to join me and observe, and the process begins again.

# CHAPTER 19

# NEVER TRUST A LEADER WITHOUT A LIMP

*So Jacob was left alone, and a man*
*wrestled with him till daybreak. When the*
*man saw that he could not overpower him,*
*he touched the socket of Jacob's hip so that*
*his hip was wrenched as he wrestled with*
*the man.*

—GENESIS 32:24–25

In the first few years of our fellowship's existence, we often referred to ourselves as the church of the walking wounded. Many of us had been pillars in our former churches. We had taught Sunday school, sat on committees, taught Bible studies, set up chairs for special meetings, and done countless other worthwhile activities in seeking to serve God. But in the process we had been hurt, bruised, battered, and worn out from church life. Ministering to others was difficult, if not impossible. In our exhausted state, we turned to God, and we learned to worship—to minister to God.

As we began to be healed and revitalized in worship, we started to have fellowship with one another in our kinship groups. As a natural outgrowth of worship and fellowship, we saw the need to start ministering to each other. God gave us a new understanding and clarity about ministry by highlighting the ministry of Jesus while he was on earth.[1]

John understood and maintained that true leadership and wisdom are formed in the crucible of hardship. There is an inherent integrity in being honest and vulnerable regarding our own struggles and challenges as leaders. To deny that we've faced challenges creates a chasm between us and those we lead. Besides being disingenuous, it greatly reduces our capacity to relate empathetically. Hardship, suffering, trials, and temptation are all part of life in a fallen world, and as leaders we owe it to the Lord and to our flocks to help people face and endure them with honesty and faith.

Jesus set this example in his own ministry. Henri Nouwen put it this way:

The Messiah, the story tells us, is sitting among the poor binding his wounds one at a time, always prepared for the moment he might be needed. So it is too, with ministers. Since it is their task to make visible the first vestiges of liberation for others, they must bind their own wounds carefully, in anticipation of the moment when they will be needed. They are each called to be the wounded healer, the ones who must not only look after their own wounds, but at the same time be prepared to heal the wounds of others.[2]

There is a depth and quality of life that comes with enduring hardship. We often see hard times as attacks of the Enemy, and sometimes they are, but we can also see them as wrestling with God. In wrestling with God, Jacob found his true identity. His name was changed from Jacob, meaning "supplanter," to Israel, meaning "God rules." Instead of trying to rule under his own strength, he now allowed God to rule and direct his life. And the limp he walked with would be a constant reminder of that transition.

In his letter to the Romans, Paul said: "Not only so, but we also glory in our sufferings, because we know that suffering produces perseverance; perseverance, character; and character, hope. And hope does not put us to shame, because God's love has been poured out into our hearts through the Holy Spirit, who has been given to us" (5:3–5). Paul, too, was acutely aware of the character formation that begins with hardship. If we don't prepare ourselves for this, hardship will cause disillusionment and bitterness rather than perseverance and character. This is one of the most fundamental truths we can teach to the people God has entrusted us to care for. In reality, all Christians and all people will go through some form of hardship. This is a promise (Heb. 12:1–13).

John Wimber not only taught this principle, he lived it. Beyond his ongoing health issues, he also dealt with criticism throughout much of his pastorate. Despite those things, plus the deaths of some of his dearest friends and colleagues, including

Brent Rue and David Watson, he limped on. John was open about his own hardships, creating an environment of freedom to not only be honest about our struggles but also to fall short. He ingrained this in the lives of those he mentored and continually challenged us to get our life, identity, and worth from Christ and not our ministry.

In the Winter 1989 issue of *Equipping the Saints* John wrote:

> All too often in my counseling with young pastors I have found that they become so wrapped up in their quest for success, advancement, and visibility that they have little understanding how to serve God in a hidden, humble way. Like Peter, they serve a god of their own making—the triumphant god of success, not the suffering servant of the cross. They don't understand that at its most fundamental point ministry involves faithfulness and humility of heart and mind.[3]

Five years later he wrote: "We conceive in our philosophy, leadership not as a position, a title, power, authority, respect or privilege . . . but an obligation to service and self-sacrifice. There's a difference between structural authority (in which one has all the aforementioned) and spiritual authority based on attitude, character, gifting and anointing."[4]

John recognized that while gifting and anointing come from God, attitude and character are forged in leaders' lives as they go through challenges. This is another leadership lesson for which I'm personally indebted to John. Ministry has never been easy. I believe that one reason so many pastoral leaders leave is that they are disillusioned and weren't adequately prepared for the challenges. In fact, many of the thirty-four years I've been in ministry have been difficult. But through it all I've never doubted that God was with me and for me. Furthermore, I was never disillusioned when things were difficult because that was what I expected. This lesson has proven invaluable over the years. For that, I am continually grateful.

# CHAPTER 20

# THE DEVIL NEVER
# TAKES A DAY OFF

*Be alert and of sober mind. Your enemy*
*the devil prowls around like a roaring lion*
*looking for someone to devour.*
—1 PETER 5:8

Spiritual warfare is one of the inconvenient truths of kingdom living and kingdom ministry. Our Enemy, the devil, would like nothing more than to make us lax and unfocused in our commission to make disciples. He will use whatever means he can to distract us, scare us, dissuade us, or otherwise take us out of the game. As John was fond of saying, "The devil never takes a day off." Jesus and the Father are always at work, but so is the devil. Peter's exhortation was to be alert. Over time we develop an awareness that helps us to recognize the Enemy's attacks before they bear demonic and detrimental fruit in our lives. John helped increase that awareness by teaching about worldview.

Worldview, he said, is a lens through which we see and evaluate the world around us—a paradigm, a way of understanding and processing things. Most of us raised in the twentieth or twenty-first centuries have a Western rational worldview that excludes the supernatural. People are inclined to believe in angels because, well, they're beautiful and kind and are sometimes depicted as chubby babies.

But the devil and demons—that's another story! Harry Blamires wrote: "A prime mark of the Christian mind is it cultivates the eternal perspective. It is supernaturally oriented and brings to bear upon earthly considerations the fact of heaven and the fact of hell."[1] John taught that a worldview informed by the Bible and reflecting the kingdom of God will embrace the supernatural. It will include an understanding of supernatural beings, both angelic and demonic, and of a God who speaks and actively intervenes in the affairs of men. A God who heals. A God of deliverance, miracles, and the gifts of the Spirit.

A kingdom worldview includes an acute and sensitive awareness of the power and spread of evil. It also acknowledges that suffering is a central theme in Scripture and a reality in life. A worldview that is biblically framed and kingdom minded will illustrate real life and comprehend our brokenness and suffering.

John believed that while the Enemy is wily and continually morphs and updates his ploys, he really isn't creative and uses the same approaches he has always used. In the garden of Eden he questioned Eve, "Did God really say that?" It worked. And that line has been working well ever since. What John taught about spiritual warfare is much more complex than can be covered in this book; however, one of the chief battlegrounds is clearly the believer's mind. The devil will often try to sow doubt into our thinking by causing us to question what God has said. If he can get us to doubt God's Word, whether written in Scripture or a word of direction God has spoken to us by other means, he will effectively disable us.

This is why Paul is so adamant about controlling our thought processes. "We demolish arguments and every pretension that sets itself up against the knowledge of God, and we take captive every thought to make it obedient to Christ" (2 Cor. 10:5). "Finally, brothers and sisters, whatever is true, whatever is noble, whatever is right, whatever is pure, whatever is lovely, whatever is admirable—if anything is excellent or praiseworthy—think about such things" (Phil. 4:8).

John knew that all ministry begins with an idea, a vision, a plan. If the devil can interrupt ministry at that stage, he's already won the battle. Frank Laubach, Brother Andrew's coauthor for *Practicing His Presence*, proposes a "game with minutes." In it we endeavor to think of Christ at least once each minute. In his 1953 essay "The Game with Minutes," Laubach wrote:

> Experience has told us that good resolutions are not enough. We need to discipline our lives to an ordered regime. The "Game with Minutes" is a rather lighthearted name for such a regime in the realm of the spirit. Many of us have found it to be enormously helpful. It is a new name for something as old as Enoch, who "walked with God." It is a way of living which nearly everybody knows and nearly everybody

had ignored. Students will at once recognize it as a fresh approach to Brother Lawrence's *Practicing the Presence of God*.[2]

Most of us have a lot on our minds. We're already thinking about twenty-seven other things, and now we're supposed to think about Jesus too? Is that not Paul's admonition in Philippians? To think of his beauty? To give him thanks? It can only benefit us to do so. If John were here today, he would urge us to train our minds, shut off twenty-one or twenty-two of those twenty-seven things, and ponder for just a moment the goodness of God. The devil never takes a day off, and by drawing into the presence of God, neither should we.

# CHAPTER 21

# GOD WILL DO TO YOU WHAT HE WANTS TO DO THROUGH YOU

*Praise be to the God and Father of our Lord
Jesus Christ, the Father of compassion and
the God of all comfort, who comforts us
in all our troubles, so that we can comfort
those in any trouble with the comfort we
ourselves receive from God.*
—2 CORINTHIANS 1:3–4

Not long ago I had an opportunity to speak in another Vineyard church not far from where I live. During a prayer time before the service, I met a young woman I'll call Ann. She was bubbly and filled with faith. A few minutes later, as the service began, I learned she was one of the worship leaders. Ann led a couple of the songs in the set that morning and did a lovely job bringing the congregation into the presence of God.

As I was stepping up to speak, I felt the Lord say to me that he was going to give her songs of joy that would break strongholds of depression and oppression over her generation. Before I began my teaching, I called on her and asked if I could share something. She responded timidly, and I presented the impression God had given me. After the service, I walked over to say goodbye and she gave me a hug, and I explained further what I was feeling.

I told her that many of her contemporaries were suffering from depression and lack of direction, and I believed the Lord was going to give her songs of joy that would usher her generation into a renewed sense of purpose and value accompanied by joy. She looked at me and asked if I knew she suffered from depression.

"No," I replied. "I had no idea." She seemed so bubbly during prayer that I would never have guessed. This word had all the more meaning to me now, and I understood what it must mean to her. God was going to heal her of depression and put joy in her heart using worship and songwriting as a vehicle. Then he was going to take those songs and use them as keys to unlock depression in the hearts of others. He was going to do *to* her what he intended to do *through* her.

This phrase "God will do to you what he wants to do through you" was John's way of identifying the process by which the Holy Spirit instills empathy and compassion to advance his kingdom as we then minister to others.

This "to you and through you" principle is evident throughout

Scripture. In Genesis, jealousy and hubris led Joseph's brothers to sell him into slavery. He then spent years as an indentured servant and in prison. Finally, God freed him. When he was reunited with his brothers, the tables were turned, and he had the power to bring life or death to them. He said, "Do not be distressed and do not be angry with yourselves for selling me here, because it was to save lives that God sent me ahead of you" (Gen. 45:5). God delivered Joseph, gave him freedom and authority, and used him to deliver his family and, ultimately, his nation.

Possibly no one in Scripture had as radical a "to you and through you" transformation as the apostle John. Rough-and-tumble fishermen, John and his brother James were dubbed "the Sons of Thunder." Aptly so, because when Jesus and company received a cold shoulder from a Samaritan village, John and James wanted to smoke them.

John was an activist, a "get 'er done" kinda guy. But during his time with Jesus, something happened. At the Last Supper it's John leaning back and putting his head on Jesus' chest. John alone among the disciples was at the foot of cross. A Son of Thunder became the Beloved. Being with Jesus changed John. It humbled him. It slowed him down and gave him a different perspective on people. His time with Jesus shaped his later ministry and transformed him into the apostle of love.

John Wimber regularly reminded us that time with Jesus will transform us. It has a way of smoothing off rough edges. Of humbling our hearts and healing our wounds, shaping us into useful vessels for the master, prepared to do any good work (2 Tim. 2:20–21).

In his graciousness, God will at times give us insight into what he is doing in us that he wants to do through us. One such time for me happened in the late eighties. A friend of mine had helped out as a volunteer youth leader at Anaheim for a few years when his brother-in-law assumed pastoral leadership at a nearby small Foursquare Church. My friend began attending there to help him out.

One afternoon my phone rang, and my friend was on the line. "Is it happening?" he practically shouted.

"Aaaah, is what happening?" was my response.

"Is the Spirit moving? People here are being touched by the Lord left and right. Almost everyone prayed for gets touched or receives a word. I thought that if it was like this here, it *must* be happening with you guys!"

"Well, it's kind of just business as usual over here," I answered. "But if everyone gets touched, I'll be right over."

I drove to the church where my friend and his brother-in-law were pastoring. My friend greeted me with a big hug and introduced his brother-in-law, then invited me into his office. We spent a little while talking about what had been happening in their midst for the last few days when my friend said, "Okay, let's pray for you."

They began to pray and after a few minutes asked if I sensed the Lord's presence or felt he was saying anything to me.

"No, not really."

They continued to pray, and again my friend asked if I was feeling anything from the Lord. Again my response was no. He asked his brother-in-law if he was receiving anything for me. Neither of them was, and while I felt blessed that they were willing to take the time to pray with me, the experience wasn't as billed at all. Then my friend said to his brother-in-law, "Go get Aaron. Let's ask him to pray."

Aaron! *Yes*, I thought. *This must be the prophetic guy, the big gun that they only break out for the hard cases.*

A couple of minutes later, he returned with a young boy in tow. "Glenn, this is my son Aaron. Is it okay if he prays with us for you?" *Sure*, I thought. But I was a bit discouraged; I was expecting a wild-eyed prophet with flowing hair that was glowing a la Charlton Heston in *The Ten Commandments*, not a six-year-old.

Again the guys began to pray, and after a while my friend asked, "Aaron, is Jesus showing you anything for Pastor Glenn?"

"Yes," he replied. "He has a blue ribbon in front of him, like the one Charlotte (of *Charlotte's Web*) got at the fair."

"Great," said his father. "What does it say?"

"D-A-D," Aaron spelled out the word.

"Dad!" exclaimed his father. "The Lord wants you to know you're a blue-ribbon dad!" This was a nice word to receive. Being in ministry, I was away from home more than I liked and sometimes fretted over not being around for my four kids as much as I should.

"That's great, Aaron. Is Jesus showing you anything else?"

"Yes, there is a word written right across his chest," Aaron replied.

"What does it say?" his father questioned.

"Dad, you know I can't read!" Aaron protested.

"Can you spell it?"

"Sure, it says A-S-S!"

At this point it got very quiet for a few moments. Finally my friend asked, "Is there a ministry situation you're dealing with right now that involves a difficult or stubborn person?"

"No, nothing out of the ordinary at all," I answered.

The inquiry went on for a few more minutes, with the guys

offering up every possible explanation they could think of. But nothing made sense. Our prayer time had ended, and I needed to get back to the office, so we said our goodbyes. Both men were apologetic. I told them not to be; Aaron was simply reporting what he saw and clearly had no ill intent at all.

When I got home, I shared the story with Donna, who offered her wisdom on the issue: "That's weird."

"Thanks, honey, great insight."

A little later my phone rang. This being long before caller ID, I picked up not knowing who was calling and heard my friend's voice. "Hello. And, no, I'm not coming over to get prayed for. I've had enough prophetic input for one day."

I was just playing with him, of course, but my friend sincerely wanted to share something with me. "After you left, I was so confused. Aaron hears from the Lord all the time, and this was just so strange that I went into my office and prayed. I was asking the Lord what it meant, and I heard as clear as anything 'What does my Word say?'

"I thought about it for a minute, pulled a biblical encyclopedia off my shelf, and looked up the word *ass*. Let me read what it says: 'The ass in ancient Israel was a symbol of strength and endurance. Used for carrying heavy loads even in extreme conditions, the ass was valued by farmers as well as those traveling. Often kings and other noblemen rode upon the ass.' That's your ministry, Glenn. That describes who you are and what you're called to do. It's a humble ministry, but one that glorifies God."

Since then I've cherished that word. After thirty-five years in ministry (thirty-plus years since that word was given to me), I realize it did describe me. I learned that the package isn't important. The prophetic person, whoever he or she might be, is only an instrument of the Lord. I also learned to weigh a word on the merit of the word itself, not on the visibility or dynamic nature of the person giving it. God will use whom he will use.

# CHAPTER 22

# GIVE TO GET, TO GIVE, TO GET, TO GIVE . . .

*A generous person will prosper;*
*whoever refreshes others will be refreshed.*
—PROVERBS 11:25

To be a better getter and to be a better giver are not mutually exclusive. Unless wealth has fallen into our laps, to be givers we must also be getters. It takes work to give, whether what we give is money, useful goods, or our undivided attention.[1]

In contrast to today's prosperity teaching, John always put the focus on giving, not receiving. His sincere conviction was that you just cannot outgive God. As with most of his sayings, John lived this one out. He was one of the most generous people I have ever known. Being his gardener was kind of unnerving. I was used to giving someone a price for a particular job and then quibbling a bit, ultimately agreeing on a number and doing the work. John never asked how much something cost. He just told me to go do it and then when I was done would say, "Looks great. Go see Carol. She'll give you a check." One time he was there when I told Carol the cost, and he said, "That's too low. You were here all day." And he told her to give me more than I had asked for.

In January 1982, Donna and I were married. In June we went to England with John and the team. Later that same year he was taking a team to South Africa to plant the first Vineyard church there. It was an extended trip—two months long—and the cost was more than three thousand dollars each. We felt led to go and signed up in faith. As the trip approached, we had made an initial down payment but were falling behind, and a big payment to cover airfare was coming due.

Our friends Nancy and Steve Bray had also signed up to go but realized they would be unable to. They knew we were behind and asked their initial payment to be transferred to us. This was one example of the spirit of generosity fostered at that time.

I sold my snow skis to raise money, but we were still about one thousand dollars short. I told John I was going to sell my stereo system. I loved my stereo. I had purchased it a couple of years before, while I was living with John's son Chris. He cleaned swimming pools and I mowed lawns, but we both loved music and would go home at night and blast the Pretenders or old Beatles albums at high volume.

John asked how much I was going to ask for the stereo. "A thousand dollars," I replied. "That'll pay the balance on our trip."

"Bring me the stereo. I'll set it up in my office and later, when you save the money, you can buy it back." John and the Brays made it possible for us to be a part of a monumental event in Vineyard history, and for that we have always been grateful.

The spiritual truth wrapped into this little saying is that we simply cannot outgive God. We just don't have the capacity or the resources. We can, however, tap into his Spirit of unparalleled generosity. John knew that generosity isn't an easy lesson to learn, but it is one of the ways that we, as followers of Jesus, can best reflect his goodness.

Generosity is a key to the kingdom. In being generous, we break the grip of self-centeredness that constricts the hearts of so many people. We break free from the fear of not having enough and enter the joy of Jesus: "For the joy set before him he endured the cross" (Heb. 12:2). Jesus gave sacrificially, and he gave with joy. There are depths of joy that can only be experienced as we express generosity to others. Our giving must be with no strings attached, as my friend Steve Sjogren likes to say. Freely we have received, freely we must give (Matt. 10:8). Generosity is rooted in grace. It is an outpouring of gratitude and an expression of worship to the God who gave his Son for us. When we begin to see giving in this light, it changes everything.

John put it this way:

Giving money and material possessions to the poor and to God's work is a powerful form of sacrifice. Giving that is motivated by love for God and his purposes releases great power and secures blessing (Phil. 4:18–19). The centurion Cornelius "gave generously to those in need and prayed to God regularly," which caught the Lord's attention (Acts 10:2).

An angel of the Lord appeared to Cornelius in a vision, commended him for his generosity and prayer life, and directed him to contact Peter, which opened the gospel to the gentiles.[2]

As I mentioned previously, our church was unable to make the payments on our lease and relinquished the building we were meeting in. Our friends at Christ the King Lutheran opened their building to us while we were homeless. A few years into our relationship, we had not fully recovered and fell behind in the nominal rent they were charging us. After a few months the debt stacked up, and we were facing the prospect of closing our doors. The pastor and council at Christ the King came to us and said simply, "We forgive the debt. We'll start over, from scratch." That ongoing expression of generosity has been not only lifesaving (or church saving) for us, but it has also been a joy to them and a beautiful example of unity to the church at large. Win, win, win.

Giving to get is an incomplete equation. When we give with the goal of getting back, we haven't actually entered into the heart of God. His giving was always selfless, always others-centered. Getting is but one step in the process of having even more to give. At that point we are called to be stewards over what God entrusts us with. If we view our resources as his resources entrusted to us, it makes the process easier. It wasn't mine to begin with, so I don't have nearly as much trouble giving it away. Generosity is as much a matter of theological perspective as it is a willingness to let go.

In closing this chapter I quote Craig L. Blomberg:

Generous giving, especially to the materially neediest people of our world, proves so pervasive in Scripture, and is so often either commanded or commended, that it is hard to envision

anyone seriously studying the Bible in detail and not con-
cluding that stewardship must play a central role in any truly
Christian lifestyle. Precisely because material possessions are
a good part of God's created order, he wants all people to
acquire at least a minimally decent amount of them.[3]

# CHAPTER 23

# YOUR BROTHER IS NEVER YOUR ENEMY

*To Jesus the mediator of a new covenant,*
*and to the sprinkled blood that speaks a*
*better word than the blood of Abel.*
**—HEBREWS 12:24**

*For our struggle is not against flesh and*
*blood.*
**—EPHESIANS 6:12**

"Your brother is never your enemy" is one of the most powerful truths I learned from John, and also one of the most difficult to uphold. He had an amazing ability to differ with someone theologically and yet fully embrace them as a brother or sister in Christ. I can honestly say that in the twenty years I knew and worked for John, I never heard him speak negatively about someone. When others would speak ill of him—and there were those outspoken critics and vanguards of the truth who occasionally did—John kept silent. His attention was focused on speaking the truth of Scripture and, to the best of his ability, living it out.

John also taught the value of having an accepting heart and attitude toward those brothers and sisters whom we might disagree with:

> That's why I'm calling us to be representatives for Christ in both truth and grace. One without the other is incomplete. We must walk in both truth and grace. If we are untempered in our attitudes about truth, we will become victimizers and harsh legalists and begin criticizing people for not walking in the truth (or at least our view of truth). If we overemphasize grace, it becomes something less than godly in its character and makeup and becomes humanistic in its source. It leads to ignoring the very foundation of the issue of sin in people's lives.[1]

During the late eighties I saw a beautiful illustration of this. Mike Bickle's Kansas City Fellowship had recently aligned with Vineyard. At a large gathering at the Kansas City Municipal Auditorium, John brought Mike onstage with the intention of clarifying and correcting doctrinal issues that Mike had taught, including at the City Church. During the exchange, John was gracious and loving while standing on the truth. Mike received it beautifully, and at the conclusion they prayed together.

Commenting on Paul's exhortation in Romans to accept the weaker brother, John wrote:

> The underlying teaching here is to accommodate the gradations of agreement in faith. In his letter to the Ephesian believers Paul pleaded: "Make every effort to keep the unity of the Spirit through the bond of peace" (4:3). Unity always requires some effort. We're brothers! Don't be argumentative in your spirit. Don't focus on points of disagreement or debate over the externals of the Christian life. . . . The higher path is to walk above these things and to deal lovingly with brothers and sisters who, for one reason or another, are "weak." It doesn't mean you're more godly; it just means that you intend to be and that you want to walk in the center of scripture.[2]

Ephesians 6:12 reads: "For our struggle is not against flesh and blood, but against the rulers, against the authorities, against the powers of this dark world and against the spiritual forces of evil in the heavenly realms."

While much is made about the power structures and demonic hierarchy, the phrase that stands out to me is "Our struggle is not against flesh and blood." How much spiritual warfare would be subverted if we simply remembered this? So often minor offenses become major obstacles and the focus of our ire is our brother or sister who, like us, is human, imperfect, and prone to make mistakes. Not to excuse mistakes, but shouldn't our response be to forgive and move on together rather than to fume and stagnate alone?

In chapter 5 of Ephesians, we are in the midst of warnings about behaviors that are detrimental—to spiritual life and growth, to relationship with Christ, and in breaking down unity in the body. Here Paul says, "but rather thanksgiving"(v. 4). Giving thanks will supplant those other things. Rather than putting forth energy to try not to do the wrong things, we are to maintain a grateful heart. The same dynamic is true in Ephesians 6. We could focus on spiritual mapping, naming the principalities and powers over our cities, and pulling down strongholds—or we could love our neighbors.

Spiritual warfare is real. We have an enemy who is real. There are most certainly authorities, rulers, and powers seeking to undermine God's kingdom rule in our lives. But that enemy is never our brother or sister.

# CHAPTER 24

# GO TO YOUR PEOPLE

*The L*ORD *our God said to us at Horeb,*
*"You have stayed long enough at this*
*mountain. Break camp and advance*
*into the hill country of the Amorites;*
*go to all the neighboring peoples in*
*the Arabah, in the mountains, in the*
*western foothills, in the Negev and*
*along the coast, to the land of the*
*Canaanites and to Lebanon, as far as*
*the great river, the Euphrates. See, I*
*have given you this land. Go in and*
*take possession of the land the L*ORD
*swore he would give to your fathers—*
*to Abraham, Isaac and Jacob—and to*
*their descendants after them."*
*—*DEUTERONOMY 1:6–8

Regarding church planting, John would often say, "Go to your people!" He meant, quite simply, to be realistic in who you were and who you related to. It made little sense for someone who grew up hunting and fishing to plant in a densely populated urban area with few trees and water lined with cement. (Inside joke: since moving to Portland, I often laugh about the Santa Ana "River" that runs behind the building at the Anaheim Vineyard, as its banks have been reinforced with concrete.) Conversely, a city boy or girl would likely not fare as well in attracting people in a rural area.

When Donna and I concluded that the Lord was speaking to us about planting a church, our first notion was that we would go to Missoula, Montana. I had a friend who had been pestering me for years to go to Montana and plant. I did some demographic research, and on paper Missoula looked great. It was a college town, and I was at the time leading the young adult ministry at Anaheim and greatly enjoying the dynamic of the group. We had launched the midweek eight o'clock service. It had done well, attracting twentysomethings from around North Orange County, and I envisioned our new plant looking similar to this group.

When I talked to my friend and mentor Todd Hunter, he told me to be open, that sometimes we might think we're going one way, but God has another thing in mind. I listened to Todd but was fairly confident that we were headed to Missoula. Later I spoke to Tri Robinson, who was serving as the Vineyard Regional Overseer for the Northwest Region, and he told me the same thing. Again I replied I was confident that Missoula was our destination. Tri persisted and gave me a list of about ten cities across Washington and Idaho that had been identified as potential locations to launch a Vineyard church.

A few weeks went by as we began planning our exploratory mission. The appointed time came and we flew to Portland, rented a car, and set out through the Columbia River Gorge down I-84, headed for Missoula, Montana. I remember feeling so much expectation to see our new home! After thirty-five years in Orange County, California, we were going to plant a church in Montana.

When we arrived, we took a short tour of the town. It was nice but quaint by Orange County standards. Somewhat less developed than we were accustomed to. One thing we noticed right away were the guns in the mall window, something you didn't see in Orange County. Beyond that there were numerous coffee shops that weren't Starbucks and people dressed in camo. Lots of camo.

We checked into a hotel, had dinner at a restaurant that had elk on the menu, and retired for the evening. The real eye-opener for me came the next morning. For years I had a daily habit of reading the newspaper every morning with my coffee. The *LA Times* had always been my paper of choice. I walked into the lobby of our hotel, picked up a copy of the *Missoulian*, and sat down to order breakfast. I glanced down at the paper to read the headline: "Griz Mauls Man." Griz mauls man? At first I wasn't sure what that meant. As I read the article, I realized it was about a local resident who had been mauled by a grizzly bear. At that moment I heard John Wimber's voice ringing in my head saying, "Go to your people, go to your people."

I prayed, "Lord, if this is where you have for me, I'll come here and serve you, but these are not my people."

We continued our tour through the Northwest over the next couple of days, visiting several cities that Tri had recommended.

But we didn't feel drawn to any of them. We were used to a little more activity. Freeways, theaters, stuff like that. We arrived in Portland as perplexed as we could possibly be. After a couple of days in Portland with the family, we headed back down the coast route toward California. That evening we pulled in to a campground, where Donna and I went for a walk.

"What do you think?" she asked.

"I don't know. I'm confused," I replied. "The only place we've been in the last week that I could possibly see myself living in was Portland."

"Really? I loved Portland."

We began to discuss the possibility of going to Portland. Both Tri and Todd (wise men that they are) had been right. John had also been right: "Go to your people." Plant where you'll prosper. Plant in a place where you can identify and connect with the people and the culture. God has given us each a unique personality and unique likes and dislikes. Church planting and pastoring are about making friends and building community. While diversity is of value and we always want anyone and everyone to be accepted, our effectiveness will increase if we share common interests with those we minister to—a built-in point of identification.

Growing up, I was a football fan. I had only been to one basketball game, so while I was aware of the "showtime" Lakers, basketball had never been my sport. When we moved to Portland, I quickly realized the Trailblazers were the only major league team in town (Portland has since added an MLS team, the Timbers), and the people of this city loved basketball and loved their Blazers! So we began watching basketball. I began following the Blazers, reading up on the history and memorizing the names, numbers, and stats of the players. It gave me something to talk about with people in Starbucks and at the grocery store. It helped me to identify with the culture.

God's plan was much better than mine. Portland is home. We love living here (not only Donna and me but our four kids and five grandkids as well). There are days I still drive along I-5, lined with huge Douglas fir trees, and think, "I can't believe I live here." My kids met their spouses here. My grandkids were born here, and all are lifetime Blazer fans.

# CHAPTER 25

# COME AS YOU ARE

*David left Gath and escaped to the cave of Adullam. When his brothers and his father's household heard about it, they went down to him there. All those who were in distress or in debt or discontented gathered around him, and he became their commander. About four hundred men were with him.*
— 1 SAMUEL 22:1–2

*Come to me, all you who are weary and burdened, and I will give you rest.*
— MATTHEW 11:28

A couple of years ago, a young woman began attending our church at the invitation of a friend. Mary had emotional and relational issues that made it difficult for her to be around others or to open up her life on almost any level. Reluctantly, she agreed to attend a Sunday service. Almost immediately she felt comfortable and over time developed relationships and received some healing. I got to know Mary and asked her what allowed her to enter fellowship with the folks at CVC. She responded, "I could see that they were real people, struggling with issues and fears of their own. If they had all been 'shiny, happy people,' I'd have been out the door." Mary was the recipient of a Vineyard Value that John summarized: "Come as you are."

On a cursory level "come as you are" is a statement about casual dress. Come as you are; you don't need a suit and tie or your "Sunday best" to join us. However, it's also a deep philosophical statement about the condition of your soul. When John said "come as you are," he was breaking through the idea that one needs to get their life together to come to Christ—or even to come to church. On an even deeper level, this statement gives people permission to be honest about where they really are and what condition their soul is in rather than putting on a plastic smile and mouthing "praise the Lord" during pain and turmoil. "Come as you are" opens the door for those who are nearest to the heart of God to begin the journey to restoration and wholeness.

In the early days of Anaheim Vineyard, I was continually surprised by God, as I waited to see who would walk in the door next. Week after week, people I had known growing up appeared in the Canyon High School gym. This included guys I knew in high school, who I would expect to run into at a bar or baseball game or maybe a party but not at church. One by one, they found their way to the gym and brought their loneliness, addictions, and brokenness with them. Not unlike the distressed, indebted, and discontented men who gathered around David in the cave of Adullam, these guys were destined to become mighty men. Mighty men of God who would serve the Lord, family, and communities. Men who would stand as a testimony of the transformational power of God, who is willing to receive anyone who will come to him.

John's teachings about the ministry of Jesus often noted that it was marked by a "come as you are" mentality. Whether it was the woman at the well, Zacchaeus in a tree, or his own twelve disciples, Jesus welcomed people from whereever they were. There was no "get your life in order first," nor should there be in our churches. If the church is to express incarnational ministry, we must welcome the lost and broken where they are today. At the same time we are holding out the hope that, in relationship with Jesus and in community with his people, lives can be transformed into the wholeness Jesus intends.

If John were alive today, he would say that "come as you are" has taken on a new depth of meaning in our twenty-first century, postmodern, post-Christian reality. He would ask questions like "Is the church willing or able to adjust to the constantly shifting social landscape that surrounds us? Can we say definitively 'come as you are' to those in the LGBTQ community? To those who have immigrated to our neighborhoods from other cultures? Or even to those with whom we have opposing political views?"

"Come as you are" means "Welcome, come in, join the party!" It is an open-door policy, not a protective wall. If we say it, do we mean it? Can we welcome, embrace, and love people today in the same way Jesus welcomed Mary or Zacchaeus? This, it would seem to John, is a defining issue for the church in the decades ahead. I agree.

As I consider Jesus' interactions with those outside of the

mainstream, he not only welcomed them but he genuinely valued each one as an individual child of God, created in his image. He looked past the peripheral or arbitrary distinctions and labels that culture so quickly attaches and saw them as, well, people. Are we, church, willing to be misunderstood, scandalized, and criticized as Jesus was, simply for a spirit of welcome?

In recent years the Vineyard Movement at large has included the addendum "Don't stay as you are" to this particular Wimberism. It is a statement consistent with John's overall philosophy that we will be healed, transformed, and mature in Christ. While Jesus is willing to accept us where we are, there is an expectation of growth as we work out our salvation with fear and trembling (Phil. 2:12). The challenge will be twofold. First, to recognize that every person is on their own journey and some will mature and grow faster than others. And, quite often, more slowly than we would like. Second, and much more challenging, to wrestle with accepting people whose lives are different from ours and who may not change. Can we still make a place for them in our churches? This is a kingdom tension that we must continually live and walk in.

While I can fully concur with the desire for people to grow and mature, I also believe we cannot let that desire cloud the welcome of the kingdom in the first place. The Greek word translated *hospitality* in the New Testament is *philoxenia*, which literally means "love of the stranger or other." In a world of increasing hostility, Jesus calls his followers to radical hospitality.

The upside-down kingdom of God is about opening doors, not building walls. It's about taking the time to reach out to, to understand, to converse with, and ultimately to love those who are different from ourselves. It's a call to communion, to making a place at the table. John knew that hospitality is the welcome of the kingdom. In both real-life exchanges and parables Jesus often reached out to foreigners, especially Samaritans. The word *Samaritan* today implies someone who does a kindness for a stranger. In Jesus' day Samaritans were hated, half-bred foreigners. It was shocking, scandalous, and radical that Jesus made a Samaritan the hero of one of his stories.

Who might John say are "the others" we may be called to extend hospitality to today? Could it possibly be the Middle Eastern family who runs the mini-mart on the corner or the gay girl who cuts your hair? In the homogenous, polarized, politicized culture of the hour, can the church be a place of radical welcome, acceptance, and hospitality? Do we, Christians, dare to be different, to reach across the proverbial aisle and befriend those we might otherwise fear?

# CHAPTER 26

# IF YOU WANT TO KNOW WHERE SOMEONE'S HEART IS, JUST LOOK AT THEIR CHECKBOOK

*For where your treasure is, there your heart will be also.*
—MATTHEW 6:21

What John taught about how we should spend our money is as painfully true today as it was "back in the day." Where and how people part with their hard-earned cash indicates what they value. And it seems Americans generally don't value giving to the church. In 2009, American Christians gave just over 2 percent of their annual income to the church (including tithing and gifts to the poor).[1] At that time the US was in the early stages of recovery from the largest economic recession in almost a century. However, 2 percent is the lowest number since the forties, including the prosperous decades of the eighties and nineties. Even more telling is that 15 percent of Christians make 80 percent of the donations to charitable causes, while 20 percent of Christians give no measurable amount at all.

John recognized something that many followers of Christ fail to see: our use of money is directly related to our spiritual health and well-being. We cannot profess to be mature believers, or even disciples of Christ, if we do not recognize that all we have is from God and our money is just another of the good and perfect gifts coming to us from the Father of lights (James 1:17). Joy, one of the clearest indications of a vibrant life in Christ, is directly related to generosity. Whether because of the deceptive shroud of consumerism or the fear of not having enough, Christians don't significantly differ from their secular neighbors in giving.

In John's estimation sacrificial giving was to be seen not in a negative light but as a key to experiencing the love of Christ releasing the Spirit's power in our lives.[2] John's experience as an aspiring musician who left a lucrative career to take on a menial job in a factory bears witness to this. That decision ultimately set him on the path to ministry. And his teachings on what the apostle Paul said about sowing and reaping in 2 Corinthians 8–9 make it clear: John believed giving indicates commitment to Christ in the same way faith, godly speech, knowledge of the Word, and love of others do.

Donna and I learned this lesson shortly after joining the

pastoral staff of Anaheim Vineyard in the early eighties. When we were married in 1982, I owned a small gardening business in Orange County. I had a couple of trucks and hired friends to work for me. While it was a humble little business, it provided us a good income.

Two and half years later, in the summer of 1984, our daughter Jourdan was born, and at the same time I was invited to go on staff as an intern youth pastor. Donna and I both felt called to this and were honored to have the opportunity. It did, though, represent a significant cut in pay. New baby; expenses up. New job; pay down. Something had to give. Rent, groceries, and so forth were all fixed expenses, and so we did what most American couples would do. We gave less to the church. I will confess that our giving patterns weren't great before this. We gave somewhat sparingly and sporadically. Now, however, that diminished to almost nothing. We had heard John teach on giving and knew it was an important part of our growth, but we couldn't seem to make it work. Month after month the income and expenditure columns didn't balance, and giving to the church was the first thing to go.

One afternoon Donna happened to be at the office and an associate pastor stopped by and asked if we had a few minutes for a chat. Of course we did. We went into his office and sat down, baby in Donna's arms.

"We've been reviewing the tithe over the first part of the year and noticed you guys haven't given. Is there a reason for that?"

I responded with the status quo answer: new baby . . . lower income . . . rising expenses. . . . The pastor replied that he totally understood all those things, but that giving was an opportunity to trust God and to grow in faith. He added that giving was expected of those in leadership and especially those on staff. He encouraged us to pray and to begin to give what we could regularly and to increase that as God allowed us to. We knew he was right. Convicted, we began to give every week. At first it was a relatively small amount, but within a couple of years we were giving 10 percent of our income.

That was thirty-four years ago. We've always given since then and have actually increased the percentage we give. In addition, we sponsor a child at an orphanage in Mexico that is directed by some friends of ours and from time to time also support youth missions trips, other ministries, and individuals in need. We have never been "without." We have always paid our bills, had food on our table, cars to drive, and clothes to wear. God has never left us short. We are not wealthy by American standards, but we have a very comfortable lifestyle and are blessed by the provision of God in our lives.

Beyond that, our hearts are for God, his kingdom, and his work in our community, and our giving patterns reflect that. It is truly a joy to give and to know that we are partnering with God in purpose and with our checkbook.

# CHAPTER 27

# DANCE WITH WHO BRUNG YA

*So then, just as you received Christ Jesus*
*as Lord, continue to live your lives in him.*
—COLOSSIANS 2:6

One of John's favorite little sayings was "Dance with who brung ya." It was a simple, folksy way to communicate the truth that Paul states in Colossians: "Just as you received Christ Jesus as Lord, continue to live your lives in him." Stay with the one you started with. We tend to look for the "next big thing" or to follow the wind. How many times have I heard a prophetic word that claims, "God is doing a new thing"? John was not one to jump on the latest bandwagon and head out in a new direction. He was much more a "hand to the plow" kind of guy. While there were seasons in the Vineyard that veered one direction or another, the constants were John's teaching from the Gospels on the life and ministry of Jesus and his commitment to the "main and the plain" things in the Scripture.

Throughout the twenty years John pastored Anaheim Vineyard, his teaching was focused on the kingdom of God, pursuing healing and wholeness as followers of Jesus, and—more than anything else—exalting the name of Jesus in worship. If "dance with who brung ya'" means anything to Vineyard people, it means a continual commitment to these three things.

While in recent years the Vineyard movement has redefined their commitment to both the theology and practice of the kingdom and to the ministry of healing, this little phrase points most strongly to the value and emphasis we place on worship. In a document titled "First Draft: Vineyard Vision," John states, "Our first priority as a people of God is to worship Him. It is the expression of our love for God. It is why we are alive. Our commitment to a lifestyle of relationship with God flows from our worship. Our worship must therefore be self-disclosing. It, for us, must be in our language, expressing thoughts and feelings we are having in a manner we understand. It is, after all, our most truthful place with God. Somehow allowing us to say in public and in our own quiet places, 'we love you.'"[1]

In a "Why Do We Worship?" seminar, John said,

We have been commanded, we have been chosen and we have been created to worship. And here's where we get ourselves into the biggest mess, since we're created to worship, if we don't know God we'll worship gods of our own making. We'll worship the nearest god, we'll worship the local god, we'll worship the first one presented to us. We'll worship the first thing that comes our way, we'll worship the first thing the enemy provides along the way because we will worship. Everybody's a worshipper.[2]

Worship was the fount from which the Vineyard was birthed. From those earliest days at Richard and Candi Wickwire's house, to the Masonic Lodge, El Dorado, Esperanza, and ultimately to Canyon High School, it was worship, more than any other factor, that defined the Vineyard. In the beginning there was both a brokenness and a desperation for more. It was in that broken, desperate place that a handful of burned-out believers began to sing simple love songs to Jesus. From there the Holy Spirit began to move, and those broken, burned-out lives began to be healed and restored. Everything else we know of the Vineyard came in and through worship.

In 2001 John wrote in his *Power Points* newsletter: "Ministering to others was difficult if not impossible. In our exhausted state, we turned to God and we learned to worship—to minister to God."[3]

As we began to be healed and revitalized in worship, we started fellowshipping with each other in kinship groups. As a natural outgrowth of worship and fellowship, we saw the need to minister to one another. God gave us a new understanding and clarity about ministry by highlighting the ministry of Jesus while he was on earth.

There was a simplicity, and I would say even a naivete, to worship that was renewing in and of itself. While I love what's happening in the global worship movement today and the profusion of worship music being written and recorded, I believe, if John were still with us, that he might be concerned. Has the church at large become so sophisticated that it has lost some of that simplicity? I don't think he would advocate a return to just an acoustic guitar or a seventies Joan Baez style of worship. But I am suggesting that he and I might agree that in the expansion of the worship movement worldwide we should not lose sight of what it was that made worship so fresh and vital in those early days.

I recall one occasion in particular, during the summer of 1978. I know it was '78 because we were meeting at my alma mater, El Dorado High School, and we met there for only one year. During the Sunday night service, I was standing near the back during worship with my eyes closed and hands raised. After some time, I wondered if I was still standing or actually floating in the air. It was a weird feeling, but I was so lost in worship that I was out of touch with my physical being.

I share that example to say that the attitude of our hearts in worship was the focus more than the instrumentation, arrangement, and sound quality. There was no pad, no click track, no digital soundboard or inner ear monitors. Just Carl leading, Eddie playing guitar, John on his Fender Rhodes with Jerry Davis playing bass, and Dick Heying making weird faces behind his funky little jazz drum kit. Again, I don't believe John would in any way be anti-technology or against the developments used in worship today, but he might suggest we do a heartfelt evaluation of what worship is and ask if we are on track.

I personally believe that if anything is going to carry the church through the twenty-first century, it will be a return to worship as the defining call and purpose of God in the lives of his people. In the Vineyard, as many of the pastors and leaders age and inch toward retirement, it's imperative that we raise up young leaders, impart the value of worship, and freely give what we have freely received.

When Andy Park first joined the staff at Anaheim, one thing I noticed was that within weeks he had a number of young people onstage alongside him playing on the worship team. Some of them I didn't even recognize, and I'd been there for years. They didn't always have a prominent role and sometimes weren't even turned on in the sound mix, but they were there, strumming and learning. He was actively cultivating worship leaders, song writers, and musicians. Andy was a master at IRTDMN (Identify, Recruit, Train, Deploy, Monitor, Nurture).

As a movement, we need that same commitment to cultivate young worship leaders today. As senior pastors and leaders (and elders), we need not only to cultivate and encourage young leaders but also provide a place for them. Just a few weeks ago at CVC, we had a seventeen-year-old girl lead worship. All our other leaders (none of whom are over twenty-five) were unavailable for one reason or another, so Mercy got the assignment to lead that morning. Admittedly, she was a bit nervous at first, but once we got started, she led with all her heart and really did knock it out of the park! I was standing in the front row, worshipping and crying my eyes out, partially because I've known her since she was in diapers, but mostly because I was just so proud of her willingness to step out in faith and do what God has gifted and called her to do.

At a Vineyard area pastors meeting the following week, I shared that experience with my colleagues, and one asked, "How do you do that?"

"Do what?" I replied.

"Have a seventeen-year-old lead worship?" He couldn't

believe I would be willing to let someone that young and in-experienced lead. I told him that I believed in her and what God was doing in and through her life and was also willing to a take a risk for the sake of the kingdom. If we say we value young leaders and want to "raise up the next generation," we have to also act on that and provide space for them to grow.

Beyond a cultivation of young worship leaders is a need for a commitment to teaching songwriting. No less than nine times the Bible tells us to "sing a new song." One of the beautiful things about Vineyard worship historically is that it is theology as doxology. It is a statement of what this people believes and loves about God. If you look back on Vineyard worship music from the late seventies through today, the songs written in each decade reflect what was happening in the movement during that time. They become, as it were, a musical documentation of what God was doing, not unlike the psalms to Israel. In addition to songwriting workshops, it would serve the church well for worship leaders to reflect on what God is doing today—in their lives and in their congregations. To prayerfully consider "what is the Holy Spirit saying to the church today?" and write related to those leadings and questions.

As the Vineyard movement, as well as the greater church, strives to navigate the complexity of ministry in this postmodern world, can we not also "dance with who brung ya"? Revisit the roots of the Vineyard and, if necessary, cry out again in brokenness and desperation and seek the face of God in worship.

# CHAPTER 28

# POUR YOUR ESSENCE INTO PEOPLE. IT'S BIGGER THAN WHAT YOU'RE TRAINING THEM FOR

*Because we loved you so much, we were delighted to share with you not only the gospel of God but our lives as well.*
—1 THESSALONIANS 2:8

*Essence: the intrinsic nature or indispensable quality of something, especially something abstract, that determines its character.*
—DR. MARC B. COOPER

In the summer of 1994, John was leading a training workshop on discipleship. While he was not as well-known for his teachings on discipleship as he was for other things, John was very good at helping leaders learn how to effectively disciple. He was also deeply committed to the process. He wrote: "God is still making disciples and astonishing the world by using unschooled ordinary men (Acts 4:13) like you and me to make His name famous throughout the earth."[1]

This particular training was methodical and process oriented. Near the end, while he was talking about the four stages of leadership, he said something that struck me as profoundly important. John veered off the material he had prepared and gave us one of those little nuggets that is, as they say, worth the price of admission: "Pour your essence into people. It's bigger than what you're training them for." I wrote it down in my notes and have considered it many times over the years as I've had opportunity to interact with and disciple others, especially young adults.

It is a short, concise little statement of truth with profound implications. I have realized that what I do and who I am has a far greater impact on people than anything I teach or say, and the informal arena in which discipleship takes place has greater impact than the formal arena.

In 1 Thessalonians 2:8, Paul said, "Because we loved you so much, we were delighted to share with you not only the gospel of God but our lives as well." On one level, this sounds almost heretical. What more than the gospel can we possibly give to people? According to Paul, our lives are intrinsically entwined with the gospel. It is Christ in me that we can impart and pour into people.[2] This was an earmark of Paul's relationship with Timothy. A friend of the family, Paul had considerable opportunity to hang with young Tim in downtime: to chat over a meal or while walking to the market. Timothy was able to observe Paul's life and learn from his actions. And Paul was able to pour his essence into his disciple.

John's method for discipleship was based on what he saw Jesus do with the twelve, which, while highly intentional, was also informal and "essence oriented." Here is a brief summary of his process as related in *Vineyard Reflections*, plus additional material from the training I previously referenced.

## Come and See

Jesus leveraged man's intrinsic longing for God and simply invited the disciples to tag along and see what he was up to. One of the first indicators of whether someone will make a good disciple and someday a leader is how they respond to that invitation. Are they too busy? Are they uninterested? Or do they jump at the chance to ride along? The initial phase of the process requires some discernment and ability to hear from the Holy Spirit. The person you think might be a good candidate, might not. And the one you do not notice initially might just be the one the Holy Spirit highlights.

## Model Kingdom Living

After welcoming his disciples into the process, Jesus would model healing the sick, casting out demons, feeding the poor, and other kingdom activity. One of the best things we can do in discipleship is simply take people with us. As often as possible, when I have a hospital call or am asked to teach a class or seminar, I take one or more of our young leaders with me. This presents opportunity for us to talk (formal) and for me to model the kingdom (informal).

## *"Do the Stuff"*

After modeling, invite the disciple to join in the process and participate. As a discipler you now have opportunity to observe your trainee in action. Every interaction should be followed up with a time of Q&A allowing the disciple to ask questions, share feelings and insecurities, and talk about their experience. An important lesson at this stage is remembering that there is a fresh anointing and ongoing dependence on the Spirit every time we step out in the work of the kingdom. When Jesus taught his disciples to pray "give us this day our daily bread" (Matt. 6:11), this is precisely what he was referring to.

## *Entrust Ministry*

At some point we release our disciples to do ministry on their own. There is nothing more empowering than to be trusted by a leader. Discipleship takes place in the context of life, not in a classroom, and entrusting our disciples with real ministry and releasing them is an essential step. We as leaders must be open-handed with people and ministry, willing to give ministry away and not hold fast to "our ministry." Only when we recognize that it is all his ministry and that he will multiply it as we give it away can we really engage in kingdom discipleship.

142

## Monitor Ministry

Another crucial step in discipleship, and one that is easily overlooked, is to periodically check in and monitor how a disciple is doing. This was particularly hard for me. Often, when I've released someone into a ministry position, I quickly move on to the next thing. "Out of sight, out of mind." Once they begin, I forget to check in and see how everything's going. This, however, is essential to the growth of the disciple and the health of the ministry.

## Do Dinner

The "nurture" phase of the discipleship process is another that is easy to overlook, but it may be the most important to sustainable, fruitful ministry. I've found that inviting disciples over with no real agenda, just to hang out and let them know you care, is one of the most meaningful things I can do to build effective kingdom ministries. I love to cook and will occasionally invite a few of our young leaders over for a meal. They are always thankful and enjoy the time. In addition, it provides me yet another opportunity to "pour my essence into them."

The most important thing we can do in the context of discipleship is to give away what we have. John put it this way: "The most effective way to train and equip people for any skill is by providing effective models and opportunities to practice the skill itself." This method is behind most evangelism training programs. Shortly after I saw my first healing, I asked myself, *Is it possible to develop a model for healing from which large numbers of*

*Christians may be trained to heal the sick?* I thought the answer was yes and became committed to developing that model.

Jesus used a show, tell, deploy, and supervise method of training. After calling the disciples, he took them with him, teaching and healing the sick as he went. Then, after he thought the disciples had seen and learned enough to try for themselves, he commissioned, empowered, instructed, and sent them out to do the same things (Matt. 10:5–8).

The results of Jesus' training of the disciples are seen clearly in the book of Acts. The twelve preached with great power and effectiveness, and they healed the lame and blind and cast out demons from the demonized. The eleven also trained a second generation of disciples, including Stephen, to preach and demonstrate the kingdom of God. We must remember that the same authority given to those is available to us. "Freely we have received, now freely we must give."[3]

# CHAPTER 29

# CHRISTIANITY ISN'T A CRUTCH—IT'S A STRETCHER

*Religion is the opium of the masses.*
—KARL MARX

*He is before all things, and in him all things hold together.*
—COLOSSIANS 1:17

In response to the oft-cited criticism that "religion is a crutch," John would respond, "It isn't a crutch—it's a stretcher." He wholeheartedly believed that we are dependent upon Jesus for everything. John understood that any victory is rooted in our relationship with a powerful God. Following is one of the more poignant passages in all Paul's writing:

> Therefore, in order to keep me from becoming conceited, I was given a thorn in my flesh, a messenger of Satan, to torment me. Three times I pleaded with the Lord to take it away from me. But he said to me, "My grace is sufficient for you, for my power is made perfect in weakness." Therefore I will boast all the more gladly about my weaknesses, so that Christ's power may rest on me. That is why, for Christ's sake, I delight in weaknesses, in insults, in hardships, in persecutions, in difficulties. For when I am weak, then I am strong. (2 Cor. 12:7–10)

Whatever Paul's thorn was, it kept him dependent upon the Lord and not his own resources. This was John's experience as well. While he didn't boast in his weakness, he was acutely aware of it. He wrote:

> For most of my Christian life I have struggled with a weight problem. From time to time as a pastor, I have received letters from people admonishing me to "control myself." Consequently, I have lost and gained hundreds of pounds, all the while motivated to be a "good witness" and to demonstrate that Christ indeed is "able to do all things." On the other hand, I know well my compulsive personality and that I usually gain back any weight I lose.
>
> If I am meant to minister to people as an agent for Christ, can I do it when I know there is a blatant area of weakness in me? What is the answer?

I have come to the conclusion that this side of heaven we will not overcome our inadequacies. We will make headway in many areas and even overcome some of them, but until we are with the Lord we all fall short of his holiness and perfection. This is not an excuse, nor is it an attempt to rationalize human weakness. It is reality, in my opinion. The apostle Paul voiced similar thoughts near the end of his life (Phil. 3:12–13).

As a result, I try to live a life of moderation in my work and in all personal habits. But my usefulness to the Lord isn't dependent on my total victory. Instead, I ask for his help and continue to do the work for the kingdom that he gives me. In the meantime, I live in brokenness; recognizing that he and he alone is perfect and that I have not yet attained perfection.

Witnessing to the power of Christ is about depending on his resources and provision rather than my own. Until I get to heaven, I'm not going to be perfect. Jesus is the only perfect person. My only perfection is in him (1 Cor. 1:30). All I can do is to point people to Jesus. As Oliver Wendell Holmes Jr. pointed out, "The greatest act of faith is when a man realizes he is not God."[1]

John refused to allow his personal weakness to prevent him from doing what God called him to do. While self-reliance may be a virtue in our culture, it is actually a liability in the pursuit of relationship with God. The more we rely on our own ability to "pull ourselves up by our bootstraps," the less able we become to lean into God, hear his voice, and respond to the guidance of the Holy Spirit.

I have found this to be inordinately true in the Pacific Northwest. Not long after planting our church in 1996, I discovered that the spirit of Lewis and Clark was alive and well in Cascadia. There is a fierce independence here at the end of the Oregon Trail, and trying to communicate to people that they need God is on par with telling them that they are weak or inadequate.

The old saying, popularly attributed to Saint Francis, to "preach the gospel at all times, and if necessary use words" rings true. Rather than attempting to tell people they need God, our approach has been living out dependence on the Spirit of God, illustrating it to our rugged neighbors. One key way this can happen is simply by being at peace.

Our anxiety-ridden world is filled with turmoil. As followers of Jesus, if we can live at peace and attribute that peace to a relationship with and dependence upon God, we will go far in conveying the inherent human need for divine intervention. To genuinely walk in peace requires a dependence on God. It isn't attainable in our breakneck, 24/7-news-cycle culture, only when we cast all our anxiety on him because he cares for us (1 Peter 5:7). Actions will speak more loudly and clearly to our friends and coworkers than virtually any other evangelistic methodology we might employ.

# CHAPTER 30

# LIKE AN OLD BITCH DOG WHO HAD ONE TOO MANY LITTERS OF PUPS, THAT MOTHER CHURCH FINALLY JUST LAY DOWN AND DIED

*Very truly I tell you, unless a kernel of
wheat falls to the ground and dies, it
remains only a single seed. But if it dies,
it produces many seeds.*
—JOHN 12:24

No compilation of the wit and wisdom of John Wimber would be complete without "the old bitch dog story." He told it on more than one occasion, and it lives on in the infamy of Vineyard folklore. Here is the story as John relates it:

About twelve years ago I attended a funeral service that changed my life. Although I was there for only a part of the service (it lasted all day), later I received enthusiastic reports from other participants. The funeral was unique in several respects. First, it was quite large: about twenty thousand people in groups of one thousand attended throughout the day—mostly of Puerto Rican descent—representing fifty-six churches. They gathered to weep, rejoice, and worship as they reminisced over a lost friend.

Second, the deceased was a church. That's correct, a local church. And those at the funeral were her spiritual descendants. Third, they loved the church! None of them had split off from it. They had all been equipped, encouraged, sent out and supported in their new works!

I remember an older gentleman, the pastor of the church, at the front of the meeting who cried through it all. It had been his vision to start churches and for him this gathering was the fulfillment of his calling. He could go home to the Father knowing he had accomplished what God had placed him here on earth to do.

Pastor after pastor and elder after elder stepped up to the microphone to give homage to the mother church, describing how the church's generosity and vision were responsible for the planting and flourishing of their churches. One of the speakers pointed out that the previous year the church had started eleven new churches, and as a result of that "child-birth" the mother congregation had died. It had given away all its leaders, workers and people. There were now only a handful of people left, so they decided to lay it down.[1]

John's telling and retelling of this story testifies to his com-mitment to church planting, giving ministry away, and sowing into the kingdom—not just your own ministry. When Donna and I left to plant Cascade Vineyard in 1996, we were the twenty-seventh church plant to come out of Anaheim in nineteen years. That's almost 1.5 churches per year, every year.

Church planting was not without sacrifice. Among the lead-ers sent out were Todd Hunter, Lance Pittluck, Carl Tuttle, Bob Fulton, and Blaine Cook. Each church represented not just a singular leadership couple but other leaders, worship leaders, Sunday school teachers, youth workers, janitors, and on and on. I have no idea how many people went out with those plants, but if you average 20 people per plant, it totals 740. Several plants involved sending as many as two to three hundred people, which moves that total well into the thousands. But that doesn't tell the whole story. There were eleven more plants out of Anaheim after ours, totaling thirty-eight. Those thirty-eight churches have planted thirty-four more. Those thirty-four have planted thirty-one. Direct descendants of the Anaheim Vineyard number 103.[2]

Even those numbers don't account for any cross-cultural or international church plants. My church, Cascade Vineyard, has been involved in the Nicaragua Partnership with Vineyard Missions for the past fourteen years and helped to plant nine churches there. Multiplied out again, the impact of the Anaheim Vineyard church planting is a beautiful testimony.

Anyone who has ever planted one church knows the pain of sending off people who you have sown into and watched grow. People who you love. It's not easy. From CVC we planted three churches in five years early in our existence, and it almost killed us, not so much functionally (although there was that) as emotionally. One after another, we laid hands on our friends and sent them off to do what God had called them to do. Filled with the bittersweet joy of the Lord, we knew it was right. It was the kingdom thing to do. And we knew those friends wouldn't be with us any longer. Not long after the third plant, we were driving one day, and Donna said to me, "Don't say the words *church planting*. Don't even mention it." I knew she was serious and that I better heed that warning.

John didn't often let on that there was a personal toll on him from sending people off. His public persona was very much that of "building the kingdom and damn the torpedoes! This is what we're about. It's who we are and what we're for." But I know it wore on him.

One of my fondest memories of John is from when Donna and I left to plant. For several weeks I had asked for a meeting with John. I just wanted to talk with him about the future, glean any last words of wisdom, and, honestly, just say goodbye and thank you. After twenty years in his church, I knew this was a new season for us and that things would not be the same. Every time I checked in to see if he was available or had scheduled a time with us, the answer was no. It was weird and a little hurtful. Why wouldn't he talk to me? I had been in his church for its entire existence and on staff for more than a decade.

Finally, one afternoon, his secretary rang in and said, "Okay. Sunday night after the service you and Donna meet with John and Carol and Bob and Penny at Keno's" (Keno's is a restaurant down the road from the church). Sunday night we met, and John was in a particularly surly mood. Bob, Penny, and Carol were all encouraging and kept saying how proud of us they were and how well they knew we would do.

But John was another story. He was quiet and grumpy and kind of negative. He was quoting statistics about church closures in the Northwest and how hard it was there. I assured him that we were confident that the Lord was calling us and had spoken to us about going to Portland repeatedly. He didn't let up, and finally Carol smacked him on the shoulder and said, "John, you stop it right now!"

He was quiet for a minute. Then he looked up and said, "No matter how many times we do it, I just don't like this part." At that moment, I knew that he loved us, that he did care, and that he just didn't want us to get hurt. I will always cherish that.

John was human. He was deeply committed to the kingdom of God and to God's call and purpose on his life as well as to the Vineyard movement, but he also knew the pain of the process. He knew that church planting was exciting, that it really is the most effective means of evangelism,[3] and that it is an intensely sacrificial process coming with tremendous personal cost.

Not only is there a personal cost, but there is also a cost to the sending church. If it is like an "old bitch dog," every plant is like a litter of pups that siphons just a little bit of life off the mother. A little wear and tear, a little energy and resources. Every plant comes with a price. That's not to say it's not a joyous occasion. Who doesn't love puppies? Like a new litter, every plant also comes with great rejoicing. It represents new life, multiplication, and lots of face licking. It's an opportunity for the pups to do what they're for. To use their gifts and influence new communities with the gospel.

CVC survived planting churches. Anaheim survived the thirty-eight-plus plants it sent out and is still thriving and planting churches today. But I know in my heart that there is no more honorable cause for a church than to give and give and give, until, like an old bitch dog who had one too many litters of pups, it finally just lies down to die.

CHAPTER 31

# IF YOU STEP OFF A CURB AND GET HIT BY A TRUCK, IT DOESN'T MATTER WHAT COLOR THE LIGHT WAS

*For the wages of sin is death.*
—ROMANS 6:23

*He restores my soul.*
—PSALM 23:3 NASB

"If you step off a curb and get hit by a truck, it doesn't matter what color the light was" comes from a sermon I heard John preach. He was speaking about sin and the pain and damage

155

caused by sin. His point was that the sin we commit, and the sin committed against us, cause equal damage. Both tear at the delicate fabric of relationship with God. Both burden us with the weight of brokenness and isolation. Sin is sin is sin, and it's all bad.

God created us to be in communion and harmony with him and with others. When the tragedy of sin interrupts those relationships, the void left is filled with pain that hardens into scar tissue and mars the beauty of what once was. Not unlike stepping off a curb and getting hit by a truck, sin can happen in the blink of an eye. Often with little forethought or planning. Sometimes just an impulse or a momentary lapse of reason, but the damage lasts far longer. The same is true of sin inflicted upon us. It can happen in a moment. How many stories have we heard of those who have lived a lifetime of pain as the result of a single violation?

Like me, John loved Psalm 23. During David's reflection on God as a good shepherd, he penned the words, "He restores my soul." There's so much packed into that brief, four-word phrase. The human soul—so fragile and easy to damage, yet so hard to heal and restore. Surely David understood that when he wrote those words. If ever a soul needed restoring, it was his. Overlooked by his father, scorned by his brothers. As he served Saul faithfully, Saul repaid the favor by trying to kill him in a jealous, demonic rage. And there was the weight of his own sin, equally damaging to the soul. Adultery, deceit, murder, not to mention the loss of a child. David had a shattered soul. Yet in the midst of his own pain and brokenness, he turned his eyes toward heaven and declared with total assurance, "He restores my soul."

The wages of sin surely is death, but that's not the final word. God, in his grace and infinite goodness, can repeal the death sentence, wash the stain clean, and remove the sin as far as the east is from the west (Ps. 103:12). "I came that they may have life, and have it abundantly" (John 10:10 NASB).

# CHAPTER 32

# I HOPE I GROW UP
# BEFORE I GROW OLD

*The seed that fell among thorns stands for those who hear, but as they go on their way they are choked by life's worries, riches and pleasures, and they do not mature.*
—LUKE 8:14

*We may think that God wanted simply obedience to a set of rules: whereas He really wants people of a particular sort.*
—C. S. LEWIS, *MERE CHRISTIANITY*

I was walking into the grocery store not long ago when I heard someone screaming "No! No! No!" At first I was alarmed, but then I noticed a young couple with a toddler, who was seated in a shopping cart in front of the store. The toddler was throwing a tantrum as the parents tried in vain to calmly and quietly comfort the little guy. I felt bad for them but smiled and realized that's just what toddlers do. It might be different, though, if the toddler were eight or nine, or twelve or seventeen. As we grow older, the expectation is that our behavior will change. It wouldn't be a laughing matter for an adolescent to be throwing a similar tantrum. That same progression is true spiritually, in our relationship with Jesus. As we walk with him, we "grow up" and our behavior changes.

Everyone matures at their own speed. Some are forced to grow up too quickly. They have adult-like responsibilities foisted on them at an age when their biggest concern should be learning algebra. Others, though, just never seem to move past that stage of youthful indiscretion and foolishness. John would address this with the adage, "I hope I grow up before I grow old." He was acknowledging that doing this rests largely on our own capacity to direct our lives toward the Lord and away from whatever obstacle the world might toss in our path to prevent us.

The apostle John wrote, "No one who lives in him keeps on sinning. No one who continues to sin has either seen him or known him" (1 John 3:6). When we enter into relationship with Christ, we're transformed so that the once-normative patterns of sin become things of the past. Both our hearts and minds are transformed. It's not as if we really want to sin all the time but don't sin because we know it's wrong. Instead, we lose the desire to sin as the Spirit of God fills our hearts.

John would also quote a story from Bill Bright about the internal struggle we face being like a fight between a white dog and a black dog inside of us. The black dog is the carnal nature; the white dog is the spiritual nature in Christ. Which one wins? The one you feed. If we are to grow up before we grow old, John would say, "We have to feed the spiritual nature and starve the carnal nature."

Spiritual growth parallels physical growth in other ways. It's happening all the time, often unnoticed. Like a toddler who we haven't seen in a few weeks and then see and say, "She's gotten so big." Obviously she has been fed well. Spiritually speaking, we grow or regress based on what we feed ourselves. Look back at your life one year ago. Where were you then? How was your level of spiritual maturity, your sense of peace, and your possession of other fruits of the Spirit? Where are you today? What have you fed yourself?

In addition to the practices of prayer, worship, and study, I learned from John that mutually encouraging and accountable fellowship is vital to our maturation process. We cannot grow alone. Personally, I've found growth happens in my life most dramatically when I have three levels of relationship. Mentors and elders are important no matter how old we are or how long we've been in the game. There are still people I look up to, call when I'm struggling, and pepper with questions when I'm trying to figure something out.

I also need an outlet: people that I'm pouring in to. Part of growth is exercising what we know, and spiritual growth means investing in others. I'm currently blessed by four young guys in our church, all in their twenties. We meet monthly. I cook dinner because I love to cook. We eat, have a glass of wine, listen to some music, and catch up. Every month we read a book together. After dinner we adjourn to the living room and discuss the book, talk theology, debate the big issues, and then pray for one another. I grow as much through these times as the guys do.

On a side note, millennials are getting a bad rap! From time to time someone tells me something like, "These millennials, they're all lazy and unproductive, no vision, no motivation."

My response is, "You don't know the ones I do." The young people in our church today are some of the most passionate, dedicated, focused people I know.

The third level of relationship is friends. I have two or three friends who are peers and close both in age and in station of life. While we do share our hearts, pray for one another, and care deeply for one another, we also have a standing agreement: *I'm not their pastor, and they are not mine.* We are friends and love each other on that level. *Phileo*, brotherly love.

When all three of these levels of relationship are in place, I prosper and continue to grow up before I grow old.

# CHAPTER 33

GOD DOESN'T HAVE ANY
GRANDCHILDREN

*Even if you had ten thousand guardians
in Christ, you do not have many fathers,
for in Christ Jesus I became your father
through the gospel.*
—1 CORINTHIANS 4:15

"I think it's important to remember that God doesn't have any grandchildren—that every generation must be won to Christ in and of itself."[1] This is a quote from a sermon by John, and he not only believed it but practiced it. The Vineyard was designed to reach baby boomers with the gospel, because at that time they were the current generation. The Vineyard, along with Calvary Chapel and other movements, represented a contemporary approach to worship and church life. If the church hopes to thrive and continue to grow today, it must recognize that in the same way the mainline denominational church of the seventies didn't fit for the boomers, what we created in the seventies and eighties with the boomers might not fit today. Every generation, if it is to be won to Christ, needs freedom to explore forms of worship and expressions of spirituality that fit their culture and can be applied to their lives.

John was committed to allowing each generation to do just that. He continually made space for young leaders to develop in his system. It seems a little crazy to me today to think about John releasing Todd Hunter to go across the country and plant a church in Wheeling, West Virginia, when he was only twenty-three years old. But at the time, in the ethos we were in, it seemed completely natural. In that environment I, too, learned to make place for young people and allow each generation to engage in kingdom ministry.

In October 1987, John asked me to lead a team to go with him to Scotland. Vineyard ministry was well established in England by this point, but this was his first venture north into Scotland. We would do a large conference in Edinburgh, and then the team would split up and do satellite conferences in several smaller cities. Since I was leading the team, I primarily recruited people who were serving with me in the youth ministry. There were seven youth leaders, including Donna and me. Though we were all still fairly young, this was an adult team, unlike some of the trips John had taken to England and South Africa in the early eighties. But there was one exception: Sam.

Sam was a fifteen-year-old kid in our youth group. At that time we were trying to teach the kids about the meaning of worship and how it was experienced, and instill some semblance of a kingdom understanding of what a Spirit-led group was all about. Back then the youth were more of a gang than a cohesive group. Anaheim was a commuter church, with families driving from as far as ninety minutes away in every direction to be there. Consequently, we had young people in our group from more than thirty high schools.

Building community and developing any sense of cohesion was difficult, and, frankly, out of my league. I was new to this and had no formal training. We did believe that worship was a key, and if we could get the kids to engage the Lord in worship, we could help them move forward in a vital, kingdom-focused relationship with Jesus. One of our leaders learned to play guitar just so he could lead them in worship. At times we brought in other leaders from "big church." Nothing seemed to work. One week we even brought in a young musician named Chris Brigandi to lead some rockabilly worship. He got so frustrated with their complete lack of participation that he ended up singing "Go See Cal," a jingle from a local used-car salesman's commercial.

And then one Sunday morning it happened. I don't know how or why, but it did. During worship we would dim the lights, both to create ambience and so we couldn't see any disruption in the audience and get discouraged. We wanted to focus on what we were there to do.

I was standing to the side of the room. Our fledgling team was leading. I glanced around to make sure there were no major disruptions. Then I saw it—an apparition like a vision from heaven. Sam was standing up with his eyes closed and his hands raised in the air *singing the song*! I couldn't believe my eyes; one of our youth was actually worshipping. This was a catalytic break-through moment for our group.

Over the next few weeks, several other kids also began to engage, and we turned a corner toward something I had believed could happen: our young people could be a force for the kingdom. So when it came time to go to Scotland, I had confidence in the team members we were taking, including Sam.

The first night of the conference in Edinburgh was electric. The people were filled with expectation and very excited to have John and his team. The meeting was held at the Royal Lyceum Theatre, a stately old venue with soaring cathedral ceilings and a huge crystal chandelier. The room was packed, and a sense of expectation was palpable. Jack and Susan Little were leading worship. From the first note, everyone in the auditorium erupted in praise.

The team and I were enjoying ourselves, seated in one of the lower balconies. As I glanced down the aisle, all my fellow youth leaders were present, but Sam was conspicuously missing. I turned to my friend Dave King and asked, "Where's Samoo?" He didn't know and went to look for him. After a few minutes, Dave returned and shrugged. He couldn't find Sam anywhere. Sam was a good kid, and we were sure he wasn't up to any mischief, but I had told his mom I'd take care of him.

Our apprehension didn't last long. At the end of worship there is that moment of silence when everyone is just waiting on the Lord, listening. After only a couple of seconds, this squeaky yet powerful voice boomed across the auditorium. All seven of us looked at each other wide-eyed, and someone said "Sam!" Sam had made his way to the upper balcony and was standing, looking down on the entire auditorium, prophesying to the crowd.

The crowd erupted in spontaneous applause when Sam finished. John then got up and prayed. That was the word for the group that night.

One caveat to this story. When he was seven years old, Sam would watch evangelist Arthur Blessit on TV. One day he told his mom he wanted to meet him. She discouraged him, but Sam was persistent, and so his mother called Arthur's office in Los Angeles and told the receptionist that her seven-year-old son watched Arthur on TV and would really like to meet him. The receptionist put her on hold and returned in just a couple of minutes. "Sure, bring him down. Arthur would love to meet him."

Arrangements were made, and Sam went to meet Arthur Blessit. During the meeting Arthur prayed for Sam and prophesied over him that he would be a prophet to the nations. Fast-forward eight years. Here we were in Edinburgh, Scotland, and Sam was prophesying "to the nations." Over the next several years, Sam continued to be a catalyst for change among the youth at Anaheim.

One of John's core commitments was to create an environment where every generation could come to a place of faith for themselves. He knew this was essential for the kingdom of God to move forward. And accomplishing this involves a vision of the future and the willingness to make space for young people to grow.

# CHAPTER 34

# WE JUST WANTED A CHURCH OUR KIDS COULD GO TO

*Even when I am old and gray,*
*do not forsake me, my God,*
*till I declare your power to the next*
*generation,*
*your mighty acts to all who are to come.*
—PSALM 71:18

I can't recall the specific context, but I do recall the response. In an interview, someone had asked John's wife about the "master plan," the big vision behind the launching of the Anaheim Vineyard and the Vineyard movement. Her response was, "We just wanted a church our kids could go to." When the Vineyard began in 1977, I was nineteen years old, the same age as John and Carol's second son, Tim. I was also the average age of those who attended the church at that time.

While providing a place for their kids and their kids' friends to worship may have been the priority, Vineyard was intentionally crafted to reach a young generation. John's work with Fuller Seminary made him acutely aware that the mainline denominations in the US were aging and dying off because they had failed to adjust to the cultural shift that was taking place within the greatest generation to the baby boomers. Whether it was the contemporary, sometimes even rock-and-roll-style music and worship experience; casual dress; John's earthy, storyteller style of preaching; or a combination of these factors, young people felt comfortable and found a home in the Vineyard. Welcoming and providing a place for young people was the front door but certainly not the whole picture. John, Carol, and the other leaders recognized and valued the contribution youth could make. We not only felt welcome, we felt valued.

Looking back, I realize how vital this was to my spiritual growth. About five years into the life of the church, we had grown to several thousand people and were meeting in the Canyon High School gymnasium. For some time I had been committed to going forward as part of the prayer ministry team. John must have identified leadership qualities in me because he asked me to take on the responsibility of coordinating the ministry time. During this particular season we were using the wrestling room off to the side of the main gym for a prayer room. After his typical words of knowledge and invitation for the prayer team to come forward, John would direct everyone to go to the wrestling room for prayer. My job was to facilitate this ministry time by getting people desiring prayer connected with a prayer team member so no one was left out.

It was a simple enough task, except for one thing. My new role coincided with Lonnie Frisbee, who at that time was very involved in ministry. I was to facilitate ministry in a room where Lonnie would move from standing on one tabletop after another shouting things like, "You, with the pink sweater on, the Holy Spirit is on you! Someone pray for her now, hahaha!" We would get into the prayer room, and without a microphone or any kind of amplification (during this season it wasn't uncommon to have as many as one hundred people come for prayer along with another one hundred prayer team members), I would try to direct people that came in response to specific words to a team to pray for them. It would all go fine for the first couple of minutes, and then Lonnie would start loudly praying, "Come, Holy Spirit," and a certain measure of holy chaos would ensue. Needless to say, the administration of ministry was a greater challenge than expected.

That experience was only one in an ongoing commitment John and the Vineyard had to empower and release young people for ministry. That focus is in many ways responsible for my being in ministry today. John and Carol believed in me. A somewhat rough-around-the-edges, uneducated, twenty-two-year-old, long-haired hippie kid was leading the ministry prayer time in John Wimber's church. Being valued in that way was as significant a factor in my spiritual growth as being filled with the Spirit or being trained for ministry. I was being told, along with hundreds of other young people, "You matter."

This value has stayed with me throughout my own ministry.

One of the most valuable lessons I learned from the years of working with John, and one I encourage today's church leaders to follow, is to invest in the next generation. Empower and release young people in ministry. Don't allow the church today to go the way of the mainline denominations that are in decline and risk fading into the sunset with the passing of the current generation. Take a chance. Be willing to let young people try, fall, and get up and try again. Be there to help them up. Give them a hug. Evaluate what went wrong and go try again. While those of us who have been around for a while may have wisdom and experience, we may not have the passion or energy we once did. Allow the youthful zeal of our children, and our children's children, to carry us into the future.

It isn't about me. It isn't about you. It's about them—their spouses, their friends, their generation, and their kids. It's about making certain that there is a church they can go to and that there are leaders who will make a place for them—who will welcome them and value their contribution.

My calling has never been simply to pastor or plant a church, but to be one who would champion the contribution of the next generation—a passion and vision passed to me from John.

# CHAPTER 35

# VISION INTO ACTION

From time to time someone will ask me what John was like, or what it was like to work with him. I've often responded, "A fifteen-minute meeting with John could keep you busy for six months." He was a true visionary, but he also had the leadership acumen to translate vision into action and see the things the Lord showed him come to fruition. To me, this is a characteristic of a truly wise person.

One meeting with John happened in 1991. The church had recently moved into the new facility on La Palma in Anaheim Hills, and one afternoon John's secretary buzzed into my office and said John would like to talk to me. Did I have a few minutes?

Of course I did! John didn't ask to see me often, and when he did, I took the opportunity to see him. The door was open, and I walked into John's office. He offered me a Diet Coke and asked me to sit down. Then he told me that he wanted to do a youth conference. This was something new. We had done regional summer camps, but never anything on a national level specifically aimed at youth. We talked a bit about the focus and what he wanted to accomplish, which was simply to continue to pass on a kingdom perspective and equip young people for kingdom living and ministry. John was a firm believer in releasing ministry to people, regardless of their age. In an *Equipping the Saints* article he wrote: "Would God trust a teenager with ministry? It seems wild, but the answer is yes! Your mom and dad might think twice about loaning you the car, but God has always treated youth as significant people, even *leaders* who can change the world. *And he wants to use you.*"[1]

As our meeting was ending, John asked what I thought we should call the conference, and I responded immediately, "Doin' the Stuff!" John's little catchphrase for kingdom ministry would become synonymous with youth events throughout the nineties and into the early twenty-first century. On several occasions I've run into Vineyard pastors or leaders who report they were at one of those events and were greatly affected. Some have said they are in ministry today because of the event's impact. I am incredibly humbled by those statements and grateful to the Lord (and to John) for allowing me to be a part of something that bore such wonderful fruit. As I was leaving John's office, I thought this might be my only chance, so I went for it and asked if he would speak.

"I'll do one session," he said. "You should do one. Talk to Brent. He'd like this. We'll figure the rest out." The following June almost nine hundred young people gathered at Anaheim for the first "Doin' the Stuff" Vineyard Youth Conference.

During another meeting with John, he said to me, "The Lord

told me it's time to take the kids out again." I immediately got goose bumps. I knew exactly what he meant. Back in the early eighties the teams I had been on to England and South Africa were affectionately referred to as "the kids." Other than the pastoral leaders and some of the worship leaders, we were all in our early twenties. Those trips were foundational in our growth and understanding of the kingdom, but they were also world-changing events. Leaders like Mike Pilavachi of Soul Survivor (who was the youth pastor of Saint Andrews with David Pytches when we were there) and Nicky Gumbel, who founded Alpha, credit those trips and Wimber's influence for their ministries today.

So when John said, "The Lord told me it's time to take the kids out again," I not only felt the presence of God, but I also got a bit overwhelmed at exactly what he might mean. He told me he was going to take a trip to Australia and New Zealand and gave me the dates. Then he said, "I want you to bring G-150 and the eight o'clock worship team." (G-150, or Generation 150, named for Psalm 150, was a hip-hop worship dance team.) He then named several individuals in my group.

Overwhelmed, I said, "John, how many people are you talking about?"

"Oh, no more than fifty or sixty," he replied very matter-of-factly. Then he smiled and said, "Thanks for coming in," and our meeting was over. Now all I had to do was get fifty or sixty young people together, do some training, secure passports for everybody, and figure out how to get them all on a plane to go halfway around the world together. No problem. And so about eight months later in the summer of 1994, I led a team of sixty youth and young adults on a two-week trip to Australia and New Zealand. A brief meeting with John had kept me busy for months and resulted in an amazing time ministering and sharing what God had been doing in yet another generation of Vineyard young people.

At times John's vision and action also came with a sense of humor. One weekend I had a youth winter retreat scheduled at a camp facility in Big Bear, about ninety minutes from Anaheim. That particular weekend a large storm hit, and we ended up driving to the camp in the storm. The bus we hired to take the kids slid on the ice and got stuck in a ditch, requiring the group to wait for three hours while the company dispatched another bus, this one with snow chains, to pick them up.

Meanwhile, the church van that I was driving was apparently low on antifreeze and overheated. We had to leave it on the road to be towed later and transfer all the food we were carrying for the weekend to another leader's vehicle. As if that weren't enough, in the parking lot of the camp, one leader slid his car into another leader's car! It was a long weekend.

We finally arrived back at the church building around nine o'clock on Sunday night. John and Carol, along with a few other staff members, were in his office just talking after the evening service when I came in looking a bit haggard and frazzled. They all knew what the weekend had been like. John looked at me and said, "So, how much is this weekend gonna cost me?"

Carol responded, "John, you leave him alone! He's had a long weekend!" God bless Carol. John chuckled and thanked me for getting everyone home safely.

Witnessing John's vision and action firsthand was an amazing experience. It was also a bit of a wild ride, as during those years we were never sure what might happen next. It was fun, exciting, at times frustrating, but never boring.

# CHAPTER 36

# SOUTH AFRICA, 1982

Some of the most valuable lessons I learned from knowing and working with John Wimber were gleaned from witnessing first-hand the wide-reaching influence of his ministry. In the fall of 1982, John proposed taking a team back to South Africa. I had gone on the trip a year earlier, but this was a different kind of trip from what he had ever done. The team would go in advance of John, Lonnie, and the worship team and spend several weeks meeting people, doing relational evangelism, and laying the groundwork for the meetings that would happen when John and the others arrived. The purpose behind this strategy was simple. At the end of six weeks, we would leave behind a fully established church.

There were about fifteen young people from Anaheim who committed to go. Donna and I were the only married couple. That, combined with my being a ministry-trip veteran (this would be my fourth such trip in just under two years), caused us to fall into the position of default team leaders. Our associate pastor, Dale Temple, was the designated leader, but Donna and I ended up spending a considerable amount of time praying with, ministering to, and otherwise comforting some of our homesick companions.

The first few weeks in Johannesburg were a remarkable time. We lived in a hotel that was under renovation, eating all our meals there and sleeping there while spending our days out and about Johannesburg meeting people and telling them our story. Our only assignment was to go to places that young people hung out—malls, parks, a local ice rink—and make relationships.

We met several people who became our friends and whom we stayed in contact with for years. Donna had the opportunity to meet a young girl named Lea who suffered from anorexia and was able to pray with her many times and see a measure of healing come into her life. We also befriended a young couple named Jack and Pip who were engaged, and we were able to encourage them in their relationship.

After a few weeks, John, Lonnie, Blaine and Becky Cook, and the other conference speakers arrived along with Danny Daniels and a worship team. One of my fondest ministry experiences and life lessons happened during that time. We held a baptism in the hotel pool, baptizing twenty or thirty people (I can't recall the exact number now) we had met and prayed with to receive Christ. Danny sat on a wall near the side of the pool, dangling his legs in the water and leading worship while several of us were in the pool baptizing people. The rest of the team was standing on the deck cheering, singing, and praying for those who had been baptized. Several of them were filled with the Holy Spirit and began speaking in tongues on the spot.

Dozens of people from the surrounding area gathered to watch, and all the staff who were cleaning hotel rooms threw the windows open and were clapping and singing along. This was one of those experiences in God's presence that left an indelible impression on my life and ministry. Even now, more than thirty-five years later, whenever I run into Danny Daniels at a conference or meeting, we talk about that day.

There were challenges on that trip as well. We were in South Africa in 1982, during the height of apartheid. Nelson Mandela was in Pollsmoor Prison in Cape Town, and Marias Vilijoen was president. The racial tension and inequity were largely foreign to us. Growing up in Southern California in the seventies, I was aware of racism and prejudice but had never experienced anything like Johannesburg.

One morning, only a couple of days after our arrival, I asked Peter, our waiter in the hotel dining room, if I could have another cup of coffee. Without looking me in the eye, he replied, "Yes, master," and hurried off to get the pot.

I was mortified! I had often asked a server at a restaurant for another cup of coffee, but never had I been responded to with the words, "Yes, master." Peter was black. I was white. Peter was a South African. I was an American. The differences between Peter and me became painfully real at that moment.

Peter was living under a cultural norm that was not a biblical or kingdom norm. His culture had told him that blacks were inferior to whites. Without ever addressing that directly, my friends and I befriended Peter. We loved him, laughed with him, spent time talking with him, and prayed for him. And we tipped him well. During the next few weeks, Peter looked at us more directly, in our eyes. He hugged us and thanked us, and God's kingdom was advanced.

While it's important to respect other cultures and not impose our culture onto the people we visit, we will at times encounter unbiblical cultural norms (this happens in our own culture too). We want to confront them lovingly and graciously. When Jesus encountered the woman at the well, he challenged several cultural norms but didn't address them directly. Instead he loved this woman where she was, spoke to her, and welcomed her into God's kingdom. That's our example. God's kingdom transcends culture. The welcome of the kingdom and the love of God can be translated into any language and every culture if we follow his lead and step out in faith and love.

When John arrived, our daytime activities remained the same with one exception. We were now inviting those we met to join us at a series of nightly meetings held at a local theater. The meetings were free and open to everyone. They included worship, John teaching on the kingdom, and then "clinic time." He would often have words of knowledge and invite people forward for prayer. On other occasions he would just turn Lonnie loose and, well, you never knew what might happen then. It was in one of these meetings that Donna prayed for a man's tooth to grow. Present and involved were the three men who would later pastor the Johannesburg Vineyard: Dave Owen, Costa Mitchell, and Alexander "Bushy" Venter. All three would go on to become key leaders in the development of the Vineyard movement.

At the end of the week, someone stood up and said, "If you've appreciated what has been happening here this week, you're invited to attend a new church service this Sunday for more of the same." He announced the time and location, and flyers were made available. John and the other leaders returned to the US, while the rest of us stayed on and attended predesignated home groups during the next couple of weeks. When we finally left after just under two months in South Africa, there was an established church of more than two hundred people with several small groups already in place. While a considerable amount of planning and logistics obviously went into this, it was a very fruitful church plant.

That church was the first Vineyard in South Africa and is still pastored by Costa Mitchell today. At the time of this writing, more than thirty years later, that church is the lead church in the Vineyard in Africa and provides oversight to eighty churches in South Africa and more than four hundred churches across the continent of Africa.[1]

# CHAPTER 37

# A LASTING LEGACY

As I looked around the room, I was struck by the realization that each of the three thousand people in attendance deeply loved John Wimber, and even more amazingly, each felt deeply loved by him. The occasion was the memorial service for him on Friday, November 21, 1997. Also striking was the reality that many had only a casual relationship with John. Some hadn't seen him in a decade or more; others had enjoyed only one or two conversations with him, yet they all felt that same sense of connection, appreciation, and love.

Even then I began asking myself, *What was it about John that made so many people feel this way?* Yes, he was a rare and unique individual with gifts and calling in a realm that many of us can't understand. But there were qualities in John's life that are reproducible and from which we can all learn valuable lessons on mentoring and leadership.

I knew John Wimber personally for thirty-two years, first as my pastor and then as my boss. While many of his attributes are remarkable, as I've reflected on our relationship, I pinpointed five that he had mastered. While my list certainly isn't exhaustive, I believe it may offer some insight to skills that others could develop as they seek to touch lives, lead, disciple, and mentor the young Christians around them.

First, John understood the nature of influence. He would take advantage of every opportunity to encourage another person. Whether in a lengthy meeting with a group of national leaders or a casual exchange in the hallway after a service, John would exercise influence. He would remind people of the gifts they had or simply thank them for their commitment. Often John would reference a quote from John Wesley that he had copied on the inside of his Bible: "Do all the good you can, by all the means you can, in all the ways you can, in all the places you can, at all the times you can, to all the people you can, as long as ever you can." John Wimber certainly took John Wesley's encouragement to heart and exercised positive influence in the lives of people he encountered daily.

Believing in people was another quality that John had that carries with it profound mentoring and leadership implications. He not only believed in people but also genuinely valued their contributions, no matter how humble. During David Watson's battle with cancer, he flew to the United States to receive intensive prayer from John and other Vineyard leaders. Shortly after he arrived, Tim Milner and I showed up at the Wimbers' home to mow the lawn. Almost immediately, Carol walked outside, told us that David Watson was there for prayer, and asked us if we could come in and pray for him. Here was an internationally recognized Christian leader being ministered to by two gardeners because

John Wimber believed in people. Young or old, rich or not so rich, he valued what every member of the body of Christ contributed, and that belief had great benefits in the lives of others.

A third quality John exhibited that has mentoring implications was his transparency. On several occasions he confessed from the pulpit various weaknesses, failures, and, yes, even sins. Almost everyone associated with the Vineyard has heard a tape or seen a video in which John proclaims, "I'm just a fat man trying to get to heaven." John's willingness to be honest about his own frailties communicated that it's okay to be flawed. Even leaders, pastors, and "great men of God" have areas in process, and these don't negate value in the eyes of God. If other leaders today can learn to appropriately express that same sense of transparency, they may well see their own influence grow.

A willingness to yield to the Holy Spirit was another of the key components in John's mentoring and leadership ministry. He preached about Jesus "only doing what I see the Father doing" and encouraged others to follow suit. In his own life, that openness to the Spirit of God proved to be another means of discipleship. We were taught to be open to the leading of the Holy Spirit in our day-to-day lives.

My good friend Don would go to the laundromat back in his bachelor days. I often teased him, saying that the only reason he went there was to meet girls. Once, as he was waiting for his clothes to finish, he noticed a man with two young boys also doing laundry. Don heard the Holy Spirit say, "Tell him he's a good dad." He was nervous and reluctant to obey; what if this wasn't from God? Don hesitated as the dryer stopped and he threw his clothes into a basket. As he got into his car and began to drive away, he felt convicted. Parking the car, he walked back into the laundromat and approached the man. "Hey, this might seem a little weird, but when I was washing my clothes I saw you and your kids come in, and I felt like God said I was supposed to tell you that you're a good dad." The man looked at him in disbelief and tears started to well up in his eyes. After a few moments of silence, he said, "Thank you, thank you so much."

John's keen sense of vision was another characteristic that had a major influence on me. Occasionally someone will ask what working with John Wimber was like, and I enjoy sharing that a meeting with John, no matter how short, could keep you busy for months. Vision is infectious, and when a leader casts vision, it sparks life in others.

John Wimber was a uniquely gifted man with the ability to lead and mentor many people in many ways. Many of his outstanding qualities can be grasped and implemented by any Christian leader who has a desire to positively influence others.

These qualities include:

- Understanding the nature of influence and seizing every opportunity to positively influence others
- Believing in people and genuinely valuing their contributions
- Being appropriately transparent
- Following and yielding to the leading of the Holy Spirit
- Having a clear sense of vision and managing vision effectively

John Wimber lived his life in passionate pursuit of Jesus and God's kingdom. He took risks, challenged the status quo, and left an indelible mark on the church of the twenty-first century. As much as anything, though, John believed in people. He trusted God and he trusted others. He was always about releasing ministry, not building his ministry. As but one recipient of that, I am forever grateful. I'm confident that there are scores of others who, like me, wouldn't be in ministry today except for John's influence.

He modeled an approach that was not only reproducible but attainable and sustainable as well. As I mentioned earlier, it's my humble opinion John's greatest contribution was to put ministry back into the hands of the people. Today, some twenty-two years after his death, there are thousands of people in Vineyard churches around the world "doin' the stuff." Sharing their faith, feeding the poor, praying for the sick, and delivering the oppressed because John gave them the freedom to and told them that they could.

# NOTES

**Introduction**

1. *People v. Rupp*, 41 Cal.2d 371, Stanford Law School, https://scocal.stanford.edu/opinion/people-v-rupp-24016.
2. Carol Wimber, *John Wimber: The Way It Was* (London: Hodder & Stoughton, 1999), 117.
3. *"Christianity Today* Announces Top 50 Evangelical Books," Christian Post, October 10, 2006, https://www.christianpost .com/news/christianity-today-announces-top-50-evangelical -books-23445/.

**Chapter 3: Everybody Gets to Play**

1. John Wimber, "Power Points," e-newsletter, December 30, 2002.

**Chapter 4: Doin' the Stuff**

1. John Wimber, "I'm a Fool for Christ: Whose Fool Are You?" (Anaheim, CA: Vineyard, 1987), video recording.

**Chapter 8: Faith Is Spelled R-I-S-K**

1. See chapter 4 for the full story.

**Chapter 12: I'm Just a Fat Man on My Way to Heaven**

1. John Wimber, "Guided by the Spirit," *Faith and Renewal*, January/February 1991, 14.

## Chapter 13: Borrow from Tomorrow

1. I am not saying that prayer in and of itself is not valuable; certainly it is. However, we are called to both pray and serve. Together they are a more accurate representation of Jesus' ministry.
2. "Vineyard Vision," first draft, 2. I have a hard copy of this document in my files. It's undated, but it has to be from around 1982–83.

## Chapter 14: Don't Let Anyone Else in for Less than What You Paid

1. J. Robert Clinton, *The Making of a Leader* (Navpress, 1988), 44.
2. J. Oswald Sanders, *Spiritual Leadership* (Moody, 1967), 25.
3. 2 Timothy 2:2.
4. Sanders, *Spiritual Leadership*, 51.

## Chapter 15: The View from the Valley Ain't That Bad

1. John Wimber, "Why Christians Suffer," *Equipping the Saints*, Winter 1988, 2–3.
2. C. S. Lewis, *The Problem Of Pain* (1940; repr., San Francisco: HarperSanFrancisco, 2001), 91.
3. John Wimber, "Leadership and Followership," *Equipping the Saints*, Fall 1995, 8.
4. George Eldon Ladd, *The Gospel of the Kingdom* (Grand Rapids: Wm. B. Eerdmans, 1981), 39.
5. 2 Corinthians 1:3.

## Chapter 16: Dial Down

1. Elton Trueblood, *A People Called Quakers* (Richmond, IN: Friends United Press, 1966), 12.

## Chapter 19: Never Trust a Leader Without a Limp

1. John Wimber, "Power Points," e-newsletter, October 1, 2001.
2. Henri J. M. Nouwen, *The Wounded Healer* (New York: Doubleday, 1972), 88.

3. John Wimber, *Equipping the Saints*, Winter 1989.

4. John Wimber, "A Leadership Shopping List," *Vineyard Reflections*, January/February 1994, 1.

## Chapter 20: The Devil Never Takes a Day Off

1. Harry Blamires, *The Christian Mind* (Regent Publishing, 1963), 67.

2. This essay is available for free online. It's worth a read. Frank C. Laubach, "The Game with Minutes," http://hockleys.org/wp-content/uploads/Game_with_Minutes.pdf.

## Chapter 22: Give to Get, to Give, to Get, to Give . . .

1. Miraslov Volf, *Free of Charge* (Grand Rapids: Zondervan, 2005), 58.

2. John Wimber and Kevin Springer, *Power Points* (New York: Harper Collins, 1991), 122.

3. Craig L. Blomberg, *Christians in an Age of Wealth: A Biblical Theology of Stewardship* (Nashville: Zondervan, 2013), 119.

## Chapter 23: Your Brother Is Never Your Enemy

1. John Wimber, "Calling the Church to a Loving and Accepting Attitude: Part 2," *Vineyard Reflections*, May/June 1995, 1.

2. Wimber, "Calling the Church."

## Chapter 26: If You Want to Know Where Someone's Heart Is, Just Look at Their Checkbook

1. Blomberg, *Christians In an Age of Wealth*, 24.

2. Wimber and Springer, *Power Points*, 120.

## Chapter 27: Dance with Who Brung Ya

1. "Vineyard Vision," first draft, 1.

2. Andy Park, Lester Ruth, Cindy Rethmeier, *Worshipping with the Anaheim Vineyard* (Grand Rapids: Eerdmans, 2016), 102.

3. John Wimber, "Power Points," e-newsletter, 2001.

## Chapter 28: Pour Your Essence into People. It's Bigger than What You're Training Them For

1. John Wimber, *Vineyard Reflections*, August/September 1993, 1.
2. Galatians 2:20.
3. John Wimber, "Power Points," e-newsletter, October 3, 2003.

## Chapter 29: Christianity Isn't a Crutch—It's a Stretcher

1. John Wimber, "Power Points," e-newsletter, November 19, 2001.

## Chapter 30: Like an Old Bitch Dog Who Had One Too Many Litters of Pups, That Mother Church Finally Just Lay Down and Died

1. John Wimber, "Power Points," e-newsletter, November 13, 2001. I can't recall the year he originally told the story, but it had to be in the early eighties.
2. Much thanks to the Vineyard national office for helping me dig up this information.
3. John quoted this often. It originally comes from C. Peter Wagner.

## Chapter 33: God Doesn't Have Any Grandchildren

1. Quote from a sermon by John in 1978 or 1979 as documented in Andy Park, Lester Ruth, Cindy Rethmeier, *Worshipping with the Anaheim Vineyard* (Grand Rapids: Eerdmans, 2016), 105.

## Chapter 35: Vision into Action

1. John Wimber, "Unleashing Youth," *Equipping the Saints*, Summer 1992, 4.

## Chapter 36: South Africa, 1982

1. "Sub-Saharan Africa: About Our Region," Vineyard Missions (website), Vineyard USA, http://www.vineyardmissions.org /subsaharanafrica.

# ABOUT THE AUTHOR

Glenn Schroder has been part of the Vineyard movement since 1976 when he started attending a little home group in Yorba Linda, California, that eventually became the Anaheim Vineyard. He and his wife, Donna, had the opportunity to travel with John Wimber on multiple occasions. Glenn was not only involved in the Anaheim Vineyard for John Wimber's entire twenty years as pastor, he was John's landscaper and later served on staff with him for thirteen years. He is currently the Regional Coordinator for Vineyard Missions USA in Mexico and Central America and pastors Cascade Vineyard Church in Portland, Oregon. He and Donna have four adult children and five grandchildren, all of whom live in the Portland area.